DARE TO THINK PURPLE

Joanna,
 Keep daring!
 The best is yet
 to come.

DARE TO THINK PURPLE

A SURVIVAL GUIDE FOR WOMEN IN SOCIAL ENTREPRENEURSHIP

BY DANIELLE KRISTINE TOUSSAINT

NEW DEGREE PRESS

COPYRIGHT © 2021 DANIELLE KRISTINE TOUSSAINT

DARE TO THINK PURPLE

ISBN   978-1-63676-531-0 *Paperback*

             978-1-63676-073-5 *Kindle Ebook*

             978-1-63676-074-2 *Ebook*

This book is dedicated to Holdjiny.
Staying married and in love is the most
daring undertaking of my life,
and I'm blessed to be your partner in this endeavor.

CONTENTS

———

INTRODUCTION

———

Let's play a game, shall we? We will use our imagination and pretend we are an eight-year-old in third grade. We've just been dropped off in front of our elementary school this morning. Instead of heading to our classroom, we take a detour to the front office. Today, like most days, we are sporting our favorite pink sneakers and Lisa Frank accessories. We sit for a few minutes in the front office, not because we're in trouble but because we're waiting to ask the principal something. This meeting is unscheduled and unexpected.

Yesterday our teacher, Miss Castaldi, announced she was retiring at the end of the school year. It only seems right that we should celebrate her in some way. She's unmistakable for her quirks, standing about as tall as she does wide and usually donning bright lipstick that often gets stained on her two front teeth. Her favorite part of the day is singing a patriotic song for the class after the pledge each morning, which is okay because she has a beautiful voice. It's her warmth, though, that makes her unforgettable. She gives the best hugs, her smile is sincere, and her laughter is contagious. Here we are at the principal's office asking permission for the class to throw a party for her. The answer should be "no." We are, after all, eight years old in the third grade, and we have no job or formal authority. To our surprise, Mr. Malaspina says yes, so the party is on.

Over the next few weeks, we get everyone in our immediate world involved. Ms. D'Angelo, the art teacher, repurposes her lessons so we can make cards and decorations. Our parents agree to supply the snacks because what's a party without the snacks? Miss Honeysett, the librarian's assistant, is our decoy, the adult who supervises everything for us. Maybe the most shocking thing of all is other eight-year-olds give up recess to pull off this surprise. When the day comes, Miss Castaldi is so shocked she cries. As a little bit of her dark, black mascara mixes with tears and stains her pale skin, we feel a sense of accomplishment.

To understand the journey of a social entrepreneur is to understand the mindset of that little girl who didn't let the facts about her reality edit her vision for what was possible. She dared. The English word dare means "to be brave enough."[1] While it can sometimes carry the connotation of being rash, careless, and irresponsible, its true significance is something far more profound in that it denotes discipline. To be brave enough is to show the courage that is sufficient, equal to, commensurate with the undertaking or trial at hand. That little girl was brave enough to ask permission to do something that was important to her. She was brave enough to ask for help. She was brave enough to put all those helping hands to good use. As she reflected on that early

---

1 Online Etymology Dictionary, *s.v.* "Dare," accessed August 29, 2020.

experience, she was brave enough to embrace the possibility she could dare bigger in the future. That little girl was me.

The same daring spirit that led me to the principal's office many years ago has guided me as I set my sights on achieving things no one in my family or community had before. Four years ago, the impetus to launch my company, She Thinks Purple, a social impact storytelling agency, arose from a desire to fill a need unmet elsewhere. Blame it on my being a millennial, but I felt called to create a professional space where being mission-aligned didn't come at the expense of my personhood. I simply didn't accept martyrdom as a fair price for doing good work. More than compensation or career progression, I wanted to bring my authentic voice forward and be welcome in the chorus of other voices leading and driving social innovation. Having spent my early career in nonprofit and social impact leadership, it felt natural to build from my passion and professional expertise. This time, though, I would set my own terms.

From my first nonprofit job at age sixteen working for a local museum, right through to my early thirties as a managing director in a national organization, I rarely saw people like me at the forefront. As a Black millennial woman, I was often the youngest and sometimes only person of color speaking up, leading through influence, or vested with real authority in professional spaces. That was a head-scratcher because every organization I've ever worked for claimed to serve and partner with communities of color and support marginalized groups.

Whenever I did see women who looked like me leading, they were too often an alienated voice in the room fighting to be seen, heard, and validated. When they were the founders of organizations, they waged an uphill battle to attract the resources and investment that would help accelerate their missions. I envision a world where there is a better representation of women and founders of color as drivers, engineers, and architects of change within the social innovation, nonprofit, and tech-for-good sectors. To me, the power was in telling inspiring brand stories to help motivate the right people to provide support.

According to the US Bureau of Labor Statistics, one in five businesses don't make it past two years, and about 45 percent don't survive to five years.[2] These numbers don't account for the failure rates for women, founders of color, and those who are not just trying to create viable companies but also create a better world through social entrepreneurship. But try this number on for size: Black women are starting businesses at six times the rate of any other demographic.[3] A growing number of women and founders of color are starting companies that solve a social problem, and I became obsessed with figuring out how to help my peers survive their first five years and beyond. From the start, I have hypothesized that our authentic stories hold the solutions. The key is to normalize talking about the things we often guard or gloss over.

What has sustained me in my own start-up journey has been having an incredible network of other women entrepreneurs, some who were further along and others whom I leaned

---

2   Michael Dean, "Top 6 Reasons New Businesses Fail," *Investopedia*, February 28, 2020.

3   Maria Guerra, "Fact Sheet: The State of African American Women in the United States," *Center for American Progress*, November 7, 2013.

upon building right alongside me. This book is equal parts love letter, survival guide, and happy hour commiseration for those who are currently growing a social enterprise or thinking about launching a mission-driven venture. You will hear firsthand the rules, the cheat codes, and the lessons learned derived from the experiences of real women who have survived their first five years (and beyond) in social entrepreneurship. You will be inspired to keep going, to keep pushing, and to keep daring.

Entrepreneurship is hard. Being a social entrepreneur ups the ante. For this book, I define anyone whose company or organization goes beyond generating financial value to create a meaningful impact on society as a social entrepreneur. We all have much to learn from women choosing to take on some of our most intractable social problems. We are on the frontline working in communities, but we are too often just a footnote or left entirely out of the books on social innovation. It's easy to see how this would happen. Lots of these books are written by individuals who don't have firsthand or lived experiences that mirror the people and communities who stand to benefit most from social interventions.

On this point, it would be dishonest of me to be opaque about being well-networked and having an enormous privilege and proximity to power spaces. I hold two Ivy League degrees, and I have benefited tremendously from a broad and diverse network of mentors and friends, many of whom are white men who have opened doors for me throughout my career. Even so, none of these advantages have shielded me from the reality of being Black, a woman, a first-generation entrepreneur, and someone born into a working-class family with immigrant roots. All of these parts of who I am have given me a unique perspective on what it takes to succeed in building a social impact organization and what it looks like to provide real support to diverse founders.

Dare to Think Purple is the book I needed on my toughest days. It's the book I've been writing in my heart and my head throughout my own start-up journey, with each woman I interviewed, adding to the manuscript by sharing her candid experiences. Collectively, these stories provide an honest look into what it really takes to survive the first five years in social entrepreneurship as a woman. Because of the diversity of the women represented, it is a book that offers universal insights that should inspire us all.

The women I know and who have motivated me to keep pushing are beating odds most men would never personally face. These women have had to grieve the loss of their babies after miscarriages, and others are undergoing fertility treatments— all while reconstructing their identity and resetting expectations about how they would experience motherhood. Others battled to stay mentally healthy in a world where their bodies are mocked and denigrated. Some care for aging parents or young children as the primary breadwinner for their families. Others are still healing from the trauma of girlhood, unlearning limiting beliefs about their value in society.

As I listened to their stories, it became clear their silent battles were compounded by the explicit messages that nobody cared about their experiences, that their truth is taboo to discuss. Some feared ostracism and accusations of fanning the flames of misogyny by other women if they spoke up. So they mostly stayed quiet. Many women admitted to only telling their stories in the safety of their own homes, in all-women professional spaces, or at brunch with their girlfriends. Often, they would share vignettes while we worked together on their branding. These tales of personal triumph weren't caveats. These were the core of their identity and the reason they were so determined to persist. For any woman who has felt like their story wasn't special enough or worthy of sharing, this book is for you. Our stories are the fertile ground in which we grow our impact, and they all matter.

Even if you're not a woman, consider yourself in for a special treat. This book is for anyone who wants to be a champion for equity and is committed to making room for everyone in the social entrepreneurship ecosystem. Maybe you're an investor looking to diversify your portfolio and curious about what it means to partner with more women-led and new majority-led companies. That's awesome. You get the gift of taking on our perspective from a respectful distance, hearing our stories firsthand. If you take the initiative within your organization to make more room for everyone to succeed or are leading courageously to launch new programs in the face of constraints and breaking new ground every day, then this book is for you too. In the end, we are all the CEO of our own lives, and if you choose to build a legacy of service and impact, then you should "Dare to Think Purple." Hopefully, this book will help you think about what it would be like to partner together and eliminate barriers to our success to expand opportunities, wealth, and access for everyone. The more we engage with each other's stories, the more we come to realize how much we share and how much our humanity connects us.

WHAT'S YOUR PURPLE?

Often I am asked, "Why purple?"

Confession time: Purple is not my favorite color, though it's obviously grown on me. Before I was a full-time entrepreneur, I spearheaded marketing and communications initiatives for various nonprofits. Having gone through several branding processes, I knew the importance of color psychology. Purple was the right color for the movement I hope to spark.

Because lots of women love purple . . .

Every good brand marketer knows the importance of obsessing over their client. There's no precise science to prove this, but it's thought that up to one in three women's favorite color is purple. Judging by the number of women who come up to me everywhere sharing their connection to this color, I believe it's true. If not them, their mama or auntie or best friend loves purple. More often than not, purple grabs the attention of the people I want to attract, and once I have their attention, we can have a meaningful conversation.

I wanted women to know I was building this company for us. Women would be the creative and strategic visionaries helping to launch other women's brands into the world and accelerate them as they build and scale impact-driven companies and organizations. Each year, I track how much money I make and spend with other women-owned businesses to keep myself accountable to this vision.

Because the world needs more purple...

Working in social impact, you quickly realize how much politics divides people. What sometimes feels like a whole lifetime ago, I was the executive director for a statewide education reform organization. It never occurred to me that anything I was advocating for would be objectionable.

To say that every child, regardless of their zip code, deserved to have high-quality educational options seemed straightforward. I would often watch how people who cared about solving the same problems in education for the same kids would disagree along party lines. It felt like there were solutions that were decidedly *blue* and those that were *red*. As someone who is politically neutral but human-centered, I would often joke with my friends that what we needed to be was *purple* to search for the bold compromise unaffiliated with a political party, but about people.

Because purple inspires us to think bigger . . .

When starting out, I thought a lot about why the world needed yet another person calling herself a storyteller to launch yet another creative agency. How would I be any different? What I kept coming back to was purple.

Purple is the color of imagination and courage. It invites us to be bolder, to think bigger. It beckons us to stare down the things that scare us and to push forward, not shrink back. It invites us to elevate our conversations. My mission was then, and is now, to tell inspiring stories and change the world, a world I see through purple-colored glasses.

In this world, we dare to think differently, to set aside the stuff that separates us, and let our human stories bring us together. I hope as you engage your mind and heart over the following pages, you will dig deep to find your purple and be inspired to pursue it.

SECTION ONE:

THE RULES

Ultimately, you make your own rules. Here are five that emerged as themes over dozens of conversations with women social entrepreneurs.

CHAPTER 1:

BE CLEAR

———

"Lack of clarity often feels stressful and frustrating, like wandering in a dense fog or in a dark room. We follow those who have a clear vision, plan, or process, a metaphorical flashlight that gives us the confidence to move forward."

—HEATHER C. INGRAM

Being clear, simply put, is knowing who you are, what your guiding values are, and where you're going. It's the opposite of being lost, confused, or stuck. Clarity is refreshing in a sea of uncertainty. It allows us to stay the course and remain on track even when the going gets rough. Without it, we would never get to our destination. Or even worse, we might not recognize the destination if we did arrive there. A clear vision helps us conserve our most precious resources: time and energy. Some may argue it is far worse to waste money in a failed venture, but you can always make more money. We can never get back time or energy once spent.

As you let that sink in, let's now consider how to achieve this clarity that so often eludes us. It starts with asking the right questions.

WHO ARE YOU?

Sometimes I ask my clients, "Who were you before the world told you to be someone else?" Invariably, what surfaces are the moments in their lives of gentle or not-so-gentle redirection by well-meaning people toward what they thought was the more acceptable path. It's the little girl who says she wants to be an artist when she grows up, hearing artists don't make any money and maybe she should become an art teacher or architect. She knew who she was before hearing she was wrong. After a lifetime of redirection, it's not surprising many of us end up far off course. But it's deeper than that, as this is something we do to ourselves as adult women too. From my experience working with dozens of women across various industries, something happens to us that talks us out of being ourselves.

Too often, I've observed women leaders pause for what often feels like an uncomfortably long time in our sessions when I ask them questions like "Who are you?" or "What makes you uniquely qualified to lead?'" or "Why should people work with you?" Most of us don't ask ourselves questions like this often, but these are exactly the questions in the minds of our potential clients, partners, and funders. If we want to attract the right people to help us advance, we must inspire them to come along with us. The answers come from within us. When we start to pay attention, we often find we have had them all along. Take Julia, for example.

I believe it should be a given, and not a luxury, to make a living doing what you love. As an artist, as a founder, as a refugee, as a mother, I simply cannot rest until my story is no longer the exception."

—JULIA ZELTSER

Sometimes the way we get clear on who we are is by discovering who we are not. Julia Zeltser is cofounder of Hyperakt, a Brooklyn-based creative agency specializing in design for social change. Going down the wrong professional path led her to discover her true calling as a social entrepreneur. Her story exemplifies how finding clarity within oneself can be a catalyst for success.

Parents often make the ultimate sacrifices for their children, which was certainly the case for Julia. When she was fifteen, her parents, both in their forties, left behind their careers and everything they knew and immigrated with their two children to the United States from the Soviet Union. Now, as a mom of three looking back on that time, she sees it all a bit differently.

The magnitude of what that transition meant for my parents was lost on me. From my current vantage point, though, as a mother of three now past the age my parents were when they made that decision, their act of selflessness and courage looms larger-than-life, as do my feelings of gratitude and indebtedness to them.

Julia's family was able to relocate because of the generous support of a network of nonprofit organizations, including a refugee agency that helped Jewish families from the former Soviet Union. Her first few years in the country consisted of culture and language immersion, and her focus was on her future. From an early age, she felt drawn to the arts, but when the time came for college decisions, her parents had some apprehensions about whether becoming an artist would be lucrative enough.

They wondered if I could make a living, which was a reasonable concern. My parents had to take low-paying jobs to provide for us, and earning a living was a daily challenge. To her credit, my mother didn't project her fears onto me. As an artist who was never able to pursue her dreams, she reasoned the entire reason to move her children across the globe was so we could follow our dreams, and she refused to crush those dreams now that we were here. So she encouraged me to study what I loved. That encouragement led me to attend the Parsons School of Design. It was the first environment I had ever been in where being different only made me more like the others around me, and it was liberating.

The freedom Julia discovered in college was fleeting when she reentered the real world. She struggled to conform to the norms of a traditional work environment. Within a few years of trying to hack it in the corporate world, she teamed up with a friend from college named Deroy Peraza, and together they started the firm called Hyperakt. I met Julia and Deroy over a decade into their journey as cofounders, and from an outsider's perspective, it would seem the firm had always been clear on its mission to change the world through design. Julia tells it differently.

Something was still missing. Our most joyful collaborations were with nonprofit organizations and mission-driven companies. Still, we relied on business from lots of other clients—some of whose values were different from our own. Around our five-year mark, this tension became overwhelming, and we decided to do something about it. Over the next five years, we made an intentional decision to move in a different direction.

Hyperakt turns twenty in September 2021. Julia says it still feels young and fresh because they were reborn the moment she and Deroy clarified their vision for impact. Julia describes working with organizations like those that helped and supported her in transitioning to America as both professionally energizing and personally edifying. More than that, aligning the firm with her core values took them to new and unexpected heights.

Making this shift wasn't easy. Julia and Deroy worried about whether or not it would be financially viable or sustainable to work exclusively with nonprofit and impact organizations. Were they naive to think they could be so choosey? What became clear, though, was there really wasn't any other viable choice. Julia knew who she was and whose daughter she was. Her own parents' fearless pursuit of opportunity, their willingness to wade into the unknown with a belief something great was on the other side, was a powerful motivator in the determination to steer her ship toward alignment with her core values. She hasn't looked back. Not only that, but she also looks forward to a future for her own children where they won't even have to make such a choice.

My husband and I often discuss our hopes and our dreams for our children, the way I imagine my parents must have discussed my brother and me. We don't worry about whether or not they'll have the opportunities to pursue their passions. That feels like a given, but we know it's actually a privilege. I believe it should be a given, and not a luxury, to make a living doing what you love.

For Julia, design is a form of advocacy. By helping organizations tell their stories through stunning visuals and provocative digital experiences, she helps them grow their revenue, connect with supporters, and ultimately amplify their causes. All of this is possible because she pursued her dreams and stayed true to her passions. It's possible for you too. To be values-driven, though, you have to know what your values are.

WHAT ARE YOUR GUIDING VALUES?

"I feel very lucky I get to work with two of my best friends. We work crazy hours some days, but it always feels like play. This sense of friendship even extends to our clientele, as clients become co-creators, and part of what we like to call our 'team of angels,' who help support large events and productions."

—ERICA TAYLOR-HASKINS

When we are out of alignment with our values, we feel it. When we are clear on what guides us, we show up as our full selves—authentic and powerful. We are led by an internal compass, which means we make decisions with greater ease. We are grounded, and other people will sense this about us. Mostly, though, being clear on the values guiding us all along helps us when challenges arise because it helps us find our way and stay the course.

My first Amtrak ride was from Union Station in New Haven, Connecticut, to Penn Station in New York City to attend the annual leadership conference hosted by the Jackie Robinson Foundation. On a Friday afternoon, I met my friends Mike and Lauren, who were also scholars, at the front gate of what is known to Yale undergrads as "Old Campus." We hailed a cab and headed off together for what would become one of our most valued annual traditions.

Established in 1972 by visionary philanthropist Rachel Robinson, in memory and honor of her legendary husband Jackie Robinson, the foundation provided substantial scholarships over four years and invested heavily in personal and professional development. Everything about being a scholar felt special, from the selection process to the welcome receptions. Many of us had stiff competition in our high schools and often felt like nothing we did was enough because there was always someone somewhere else outdoing us. We carried that pressure with us onto campuses where it was easy to feel unimpressive in a sea of excellence. I know I wasn't alone worrying about how I would fare in much larger institutions where not many people looked like me.

Growing up, I wasn't aware of class differences. I felt spoiled in love, and my parents worked really hard to give my brother and me what we needed and most of the things we wanted. My mom and dad were both known for being generous, and from a young age, I knew it was important to share with people who had less. College was a rude awakening. It didn't take long to figure out what generational wealth was and to understand my family didn't have it. I felt this difference most acutely when I was in new spaces, like walking through the grand halls of the Waldorf Astoria dressed in a formal gown, headed to the annual Jackie Robinson Foundation banquet as a freshman scholar. By senior year, something that had initially seemed so intimidating now felt routine. Gone were the questions of whether I belonged or any hint of insecurity. I had gotten comfortable, and actually quite good, at networking with anyone in any room.

Looking back, it was those early professional development experiences that prepared me to successfully navigate my career and later entrepreneurship, where so much opportunity is still locked away in closed spaces guarded by gatekeepers. My heart bursts with admiration and appreciation when I think of Rachel Robinson and her daughter Sharon Robinson. Scholars and alumni felt their loving presence. Through the community they nurtured, I learned I was not alone, and I gained a forever family, many of whom I call on to this day. Erica Taylor-Haskins and I met as freshwomen before her name had a hyphen at what was our first of many networking weekends, and we've tried not to miss them since. Her attendance record is better than mine. Watching her build a company over the past decade has been instructive for me in the power of being values-led.

For Erica, it all started over drinks. She and her two friends, Liz and Adette, met in college when they sang together in GW Vibes, a student-led acapella group at their alma mater, George Washington University. Their friendship had always been fun and easy. A few years out of college, all three women lived in New York City and led very busy adult lives with real jobs, committed relationships, and rent to worry about making. At some point, they started getting together routinely for happy hour after work. On these occasions, they did what girlfriends do over drinks: catch up and commiserate.

During one of their usual meetups in 2010, they chatted about their careers and discovered they were all longing to get back the creative spark they had shared during college. Liz was recently married, and the experience of planning her wedding had started her dreaming about the possibility of curating unique, beautiful events for a living. By the end of that conversation, their experience design company, TINSEL, was born.

Over a decade later, Erica credits their bond of friendship as the glue that has kept them together and sustained their thriving business. They fiercely protect each other and their team's psychological freedom, nurturing a community of support where dreaming was always possible. They endeavor to closely curate their community of partners with people who understand the power of friendship. Their team is a wildly diverse tapestry of humans from all walks of life, and diversity and inclusion have always been the cornerstones of their hiring and team-building approach. They didn't explicitly discuss being a social justice brand, though they were disrupters from the start. The founding team looked radically different from most in their industry. An all-woman trio who identifies as Black, White, and Latinx have, by their very decision to work together and share power, been a challenge to the status quo.

Everything about how they run the company underscores their commitment to standing up for what they believe and speaking up, from using their social media platforms to support legislation to donating a portion of their profits back to causes and charities. This has paid off because they stand out unmistakably from a sea of cookie-cutter teams, and their creative range makes them a sought-out partner by the big-name people like Serena Williams and companies like Condé Nast. It's not been all fun and games, but it has felt joyful even during difficult moments because of the team's connection. Reflecting on her journey, Erica says, "I feel very lucky I get to work with two of my best friends. We work crazy hours some days, but it always feels like play. This sense of friendship even extends to our clientele, as clients become co-creators, and part of what we like to call our 'team of angels,' who help support large events and productions."

Not every entrepreneur will have the opportunity to work with the people who know her deeply and love her. Still, it's imperative that every founder know her moral compass and then surround herself with the people who share and affirm her values when things get tough and confusing. These will be the people who can hold space and sometimes hold up a mirror when our goals feel scary or beyond reach.

Erica believes this sort of clarity comes from listening deeply and with intention. For her, listening was what led her to recognize her entrepreneurial calling, even when it was a faint whisper.

When I sat down for drinks with the ladies that evening in 2010, I was actively looking for a new job, not at all looking to start a business. In the most unlikely setting and at the most unexpected moment, I decided to answer the call to launch this company. Looking back, I would have missed out on the opportunity of a lifetime if I had ignored that deep feeling of misalignment pushing me to explore my true ambition.

Having clarity at the start isn't enough. Along the way, things can get hazy as self-doubt and pressures start to mount. It's simply not realistic to believe the journey gets easier, that there's some point where all the fear and uncertainty dissipates, and it's smooth sailing. Erica says this was something she could not have anticipated that the fear would never really subside. It would just take the shape of brand new, often larger and heavier concerns.

Even with an impressive client roster and all the receipts showing they are good enough, smart enough, creative enough, polished enough, agile enough, and with a team of top-notch professionals powering them, it is sometimes still not enough to quell her anxiety. The fear and doubt that can cloud her vision now look like concerns that team members don't feel properly trained, mentored, supported, or compensated. At other times it shows up as trepidation over taking on more debt to access the working capital the team needs to scale operations. But no matter what they face, staying clear helps turn the jitters into mighty motivators for success.

Few professions experienced greater devastation than the events industry at the onset of the pandemic outbreak in 2020. Yet TINSEL was able to stay clear on its vision and find a way forward. They started this as friends looking for freedom from jobs where they were undervalued and uninspired. They set out to bring joy to people through shared experiences that showcased the best of humanity. No pandemic could pause their purpose. They found new ways to leverage their design talents for the public good, which included hosting and curating virtual fundraisers and partnering with brands to orchestrate a multi-city food truck exposition to feed people at polling stations in the communities hit hardest by COVID-19. Their venues may have changed from fancy lofts to curbside, but TINSEL is still bringing joy to the masses at the moments that matter.

WHERE ARE YOU GOING?

Whenever you use a GPS device or app for directions, you have to input two critical pieces of information: your current location and destination. Without knowing both of those things, the device can't help you. It's the same when starting your venture. You have to know your starting point, and you also need a clear sense of where you're going. This doesn't mean your path will be a straight line but having a clear vision will allow you to stay the course, even if you must take a detour.

You should know why you're launching your venture, and what success looks like for you right from the start, even if you have no idea how you will get there. Your *why* will emerge from examining your values, and your "what" will become clearer as your vision for impact comes into focus. Your *how* will emerge, evolve, and ebb in response to the many unexpected opportunities that will arise along the way. Nathalie Molina

Nino, CEO and founder of Brava Investments, puts it well in her book *Leapfrog: The New Revolution for Women Entrepreneurs*: "The truth is that if you can be clear on what you want up front, you can make serious decisions about what you're building and how—decisions better made sooner than later."[4]

Clarity can be elusive when life is interrupted by traumatic experiences. Gaining clarity is often an invisible and iterative process. Clarity is found by asking the right questions and answering them honestly. Sometimes we need others to help us by mirroring what they are seeing and what we may be missing. It could require we go more in-depth with a therapist, counselor, advisor, or coach. If you feel like you are climbing up a mountain of obstacles, this next story might help you embrace the journey, no matter how painful, and keep your dreams in clear focus.

"A lot of us are in such a rush to 'get a seat at the table.' But what to do once you get there? I don't think the question is if you'll get there. More than anything, be clear on what to do once you're at the table and able to use your voice. Sometimes, we're in too much of a rush."

—JAZMINE DAVIS

---

4   Nathalie Molina Niño and Sara Grace, *Leapfrog: The New Revolution for Women Entrepreneurs* (New York. TarcherPerigee, 2018).

About a year into launching my company, I received an invitation to join the Black Female Founders (BFF) accelerator, founded and facilitated by Erin Horne-McKinney and Sybil Edwards. True to its name, the six-week program helped Black women get their start-ups off the ground. The hope was by introducing new founders to the venture capital and business funding landscape, and we could build investable companies from the start. It was worth the nearly hour-long trip into DC from North Silver Spring, Maryland, each Saturday and then the quick sprint from the metro to the coworking space where we met. Pretty early in, I determined my business model wasn't a great fit for venture capital, but I kept coming back for the other women I met. I could see an opportunity to support some of them with the brand strategy and storytelling as they built their companies and pitched investors. One of those women was Jazmine Davis.

Jazmine's maturity, wisdom, and impressive professional accomplishment make it hard to believe that she's still in her mid-twenties, but her youthful voice and babyface are dead giveaways. Small in stature but big in presence, she spends her nine to give working hours as a biochemist and product developer turned pharmacologist, turned regulatory inspector. All the other waking hours, she is the founder, designer, and visionary behind the sustainable luxury shoe company that bears her name—Jazmine Kionna. The latter fact puts Jazmine in the rare category of people (only 10 percent by one career survey) who pursue the career path they dreamed about in childhood. As a little girl, Jazmine imagined herself working in fashion. Her carefree fascination with clothes and shoes didn't last long, though, and her path from girl to woman was accelerated by a series of tragedies.

By the time Jazmine matriculated as a college freshman, she was an orphan, having lost both her mom and dad within a span of eight years. Battling grief and depression left her little energy or interest in dressing up. Without parents and lacking financial support from family, she was advised to be realistic in selecting her college courses. This was no time to follow her passions. She needed to be responsible and go into a field that would pay well and where she could find work after graduation. So without thinking much about it, she decided to become a dentist and declared herself a biology major. Her best grades had always been in math and science, so it seemed like a safe bet.

With depression, I lost a sense of who I was as a person. At some point, I started to get counseling, and I was ready to feel like me again. I decided to buy myself a pick-me-up gift, my first pair of designer shoes. I saved up enough money from my internship, and I went totally out of my way to get them. After the $700 splurge, I was disappointed to find they were unbearably uncomfortable. Those shoes sat in my closet unworn for years. To this day, I have them in the box, looking brand new, but now they are an inspiration for a different reason.

Jazmine was a great student. She did well in all of the pre-requisite courses for medical school but ultimately decided against taking on the debt. Instead, the pharmaceutical industry recruited her after graduation. Without having to think much about it, she became a top performer. Being well-compensated for her work made her feel safe and successful. One day, a casual conversation with a coworker made her wonder if she could do and be more. Her colleague said she didn't plan to get too comfortable at the job because she was putting all her energy into her real passion, the business she was building in her spare time.

I kept thinking: What was my passion? I'm not sure why the first thing that popped into my head was shoes, but it was. Maybe I wasn't used to thinking about what I wanted. Buying those expensive shoes was one of the last things I had done just for me, just because I wanted to, and they were such a disappointment. I felt like there was something there, so I started to brainstorm. I couldn't let it go. So I just followed my instincts.

That weekend, Jazmine started searching for shoemaking courses online. Within a few hours of searching, she found one in New York City and registered. Then, like a true scientist, she started tinkering. She pulled apart a pair of shoes and built her first prototype at home. Within a few weeks, she hosted her first focus group and iterated early two dozen times. Soon after, she was on a plane, this time headed to New Orleans to learn from a world-class shoemaker and refine her model. But where was all of this going?

Jazmine used the airtime to think about what was really pulling her toward this. Losing interest in fashion after the loss of her parents was really about her losing herself, feeling less confident, and not wanting others to see her. She marked her journey back to herself by going on a four-hour drive in pursuit of those fancy shoes, all because she was finally ready to be seen again. She thought about how many steps she had taken, small and great, to arrive in a space of healing and all of the support necessary for her to get there. This was about more than shoes.

She was determined to build a different kind of fashion brand, one that helped women look good, feel good, and do well all at once. She educated herself on the fashion industry's culpability in environmental waste and pollution and its exploitation of women and girls, and she wanted no part of that. Could her shoes do more than just help women get comfortably from one destination to another? Could her shoe company help provide comfort to girls and women who were dealing with trauma? Could she interrupt some of what was most destructive about fashion by sourcing her material more ethically? Absolutely. She could do all of this, and she would.

It was a way of stepping into her purpose, of making her mark. With clarity around her mission to create a vegan luxury shoe company committed to comfort and healing, she felt ready to put her name on the brand. Jazmine Kionna would represent not just the style sensibilities of the founder but her selfless pursuit of smoothing the path for girls like her. Every pair of shoes she sold would help fund the Walk in Her Shoes Foundation, which would provide holistic supports for girls experiencing trauma.

Jokingly, I have said if Tory Burch and Brother Vellies had a brand baby, her name would be Jazmine Kionna. Jazmine certainly sees herself following in the path of socially responsible fashion brands like Bombas, TOMS, and Spanx, all of which have paved the way for companies leveraging conscious consumerism to help change the world. She names as inspiration Black, Latinx, and woman-owned brands like Shea Moisture, BLK + GRN, and Honest Company for their emphasis on sustainability and social good.

Being clear on her real mission has helped Jazmine surmount significant odds. With no prior experience in the fashion industry, she has had to learn as she went. After the cancelation of the launch of her first line of shoes due to a mishap with the factory, she navigated the disappointment by staying true to the bigger vision. Forced to look for a new factory, she and her team doubled down on their commitment to sustainability. This led them across the world and landed them new supplier partnerships that have enhanced their designs. Their new textile factory based in Italy produces FDA and PETA-approved fabrics made from plastic bottles through a process that is 70 to 90 percent nontoxic, meaning they avoid environmentally harmful chemicals. The factory where all production happens operates from solar energy, which means every shoe helps generate energy rather than deplete it.

The whole industry is moving toward more sustainable design and production. We hope to modify as we scale to become a company that is 100 percent sustainable and eliminate any waste from how we make shoes. When I started Jazmine Kionna, I emphasized comfort over everything, and I made a big deal about our patented custom insoles technology, but that's not the main selling point. We hope wearing our shoes gives women one less thing to worry about, and we think fashion design has a role to play in making their lives better and easier, even if it's just helping them get through the day without foot pain. It matters to me women buy my shoes, but it also matters to me what happens after they do.

Like many first-time founders, Jazmine has experienced many setbacks, and she has also experienced success. After leading a successful crowdfunding campaign on iFundWomen, a platform where anyone can put their money behind promising women-led businesses and brands, she attracted new funders. A lead angel investor helped her raise a round of investment to produce her new and improved line of shoes and accessories. She's also received invitations to selective programs like the Vital Voices Leadership Incubator program funded by TRESemmé and the Conscious Venture Lab Accelerator.

Jazmine's story shows the importance of asking, "Where am I going?" Once she was clear on what success would look like for her, she could stay the course, despite challenges. It is not possible to rush through this process because it requires time and reflection to achieve clarity.

A lot of us are in such a rush to "get a seat at the table." But what to do once you get there? I don't think the question is if you'll get there. More than anything, we need to be clear on what to do once we're at the table and able to use your voice. Sometimes, we're in too much of a rush. I put myself in that category. I was that way at the start. Along the way, many organizations helped me figure things out, like Black Upstart, Black Female Founders, Street Entrepreneurs. You don't know what you don't know. Clarity doesn't just come from just relying on what you know. Sometimes you have to let people help you think things through.

Even when we have a clear vision for success like Julia, Erica, and Jazmine, that's just the beginning. Let's consider next how to be confident, even when challenges present along the way.

CHAPTER 2:

BE CONFIDENT

———

"Fear has a very concrete power of keeping us from doing and saying the things that are our purpose."

—LUVVIE AJAYI

It's not just in our heads. There is real evidence that a confidence gap exists between men and women. In their book, *The Confidence Code*, Katty Kay and Claire Shipman set out to understand why so many men overestimate their competence while so many women sorely underestimate theirs, even when objectively more qualified. More than cracking the code on confidence, their findings confirm something many of us have long felt—confidence beats competence in many situations. Said another way, it's often better to act like you know what you're doing, even when you don't. This is quite the opposite of how girls and women are socialized, and we often become more averse to risk than men.[5]

---

5   The Atlantic, "Why Do Men Assume They're So Great?" *YouTube* video, 12:14, April 10, 2017.

We found that our original suspicion was dead-on: there is a particular crisis for women—a vast confidence gap that separates the sexes. Compared with men, women don't consider themselves as ready for promotions, they predict they'll do worse on tests, and they generally underestimate their abilities.[6]

Reshma Saujani is the founder and CEO of the globally acclaimed education and technology nonprofit Girls Who Code. She's also the author of the book *Brave, Not Perfect: Fear Less, Fail More, and Live Bolder,* in which she admits to being thirty-three years old before she ever did anything brave, which was running for elected office despite having only a slim chance of winning. The experience was life-changing. She lost her race and found her purpose. Reshma's lengthy list of impressive academic and professional accomplishments reads as an indictment of her striving for perfection and her early mastery of the rules of being a good girl. Guided by parents and teachers toward things for which she showed early aptitude, she concluded she wasn't alone in "having spent her adult life only pursuing positions or projects I knew I could ace." By contrast, she explains how men she encountered in the tech start-up world differed in the level of confidence they had in themselves and their willingness to take on new challenges, even with little or no evidence they would succeed.[7]

"I've seen countless men launch entire businesses without worrying about having the relevant training or expertise. Jack Dorsey, a cofounder of Twitter, started Square because he was curious about

---

6   Katty Kay and Claire Shipman, *The Confidence Code* (New York: HarperCollins Publishers, 2014, 54).

7   Reshma Saujani, *Brave, Not Perfect: Fear Less, Fail More, Live Bolder* (New York: Penguin Random House, 2019, 79).

finding a way to make payments easier, not because he was knowl-edgeable about mobile payment. He had no experience building a financial services company, but that didn't stand in his way."

Saujani provides a litany of other examples of women doubt-ing their abilities despite all the reasonable proof pointing to their preparedness and men moving forward confidently and unfazed by any disadvantage or doubt. Ultimately, she urges us to "choose failure or at least the potential for it." The road to confidence starts with a choice to be okay with failing, failing big, and maybe not even moving forward.

Confidence is both a practice and a pursuit. Over many con-versations with women who are at various stages of building their companies and organizations, what I observe is a lack of confidence masquerading as many other things. Quite often, when I start working with a new client, she is looking for the right words, the right way of showing up to make others believe her and invest in her. She wants to stand more confidently in her own story and thinks if she can just find the perfect words, the confidence will follow.

Every woman I've ever coached soon learns that, with few exceptions, any words said with confidence are the right words. This doesn't mean we wasted our time together spent crafting their executive and brand stories. It's just to say that in the practice of speaking their authentic truths aloud, they often discover what they have wanted to say all along. The more con-fident we become in sharing our story, the more powerfully our words land on the ears of those listening to them. It becomes a generous and virtuous cycle where with each decision to practice confidence, we become more confident.

Where, when, and how do we learn to shrink, to hide, and to doubt? Are there clues in the experiences of other women that can help us find our way back to ourselves and become more confident? I would say for girls, there is an invisible curriculum that teaches us to derive our value from external things, validating ourselves by how others perceive us, and this pressure remains on us as a mold, shaping us from girlhood, through adolescence, and reinforces throughout our adulthood.

We become more confident by letting go of the things that would otherwise diminish our self-belief, being mindful of the messages we internalize, and remembering all we've already overcome to help us stand tall in the moments when we feel a temptation to shrink. Laura, Roshawnna, and Clarissa's stories leave us clues for how to uncover the confidence we have intrinsically and to leverage it as we pursue our greater impact.

UNBURDEN YOURSELF OF UNFAIR EXPECTATIONS

"I don't have to walk any other path but my own. I don't have to look like, speak like, act like, or lead like anyone else. I get to be confident not because of something I've accomplished, but simply because I am being myself and nothing else. And you get to do the same."

—LAURA DONALD

With those bold words, Laura Donald concluded her talk at She Thinks Purple's first-ever female founder storytelling showcase. Laura is the founder and CEO of Axis Talent Partners, an executive search and talent strategy firm that partners with social impact organizations exclusively and centers on equity and inclusivity. Laura speaks with a singsong and bright cadence. Her voice feels the way sunshine does when it hits your face in the morning, warm and welcoming. Get her talking about injustice, racial equity, income disparities, or anything related to America's legacy of slavery, and that warmth becomes a fiery haze. Her mama-bear defenses come alive when she discusses her hopes for her children and our collective future. She is confident in her vision for building a different kind of talent recruitment firm that doesn't just talk the talk but takes meaningful action to shift the nonprofit and social impact sector for good. Like many women, Laura struggled with confidence. She learned to be confident through a series of unanticipated and unfortunate life events.

Nobody knew me as a brand strategist, executive storytelling coach, or social entrepreneur when I started in 2017. Sure, I had gotten good at weaving narratives through my work leading nonprofit communications teams and projects, but this was different. I decided that the best way to introduce my start-up to the world was to host a showcase of female founders and show my capabilities to a broader audience. I enlisted seven women who were my ideal clients and provided them storytelling coaching for free, and my only ask was that they share their stories on stage in front of a bunch of people.

For this first Female Founder's Storytelling Showcase, I anticipated an intimate event of about fifty women, but it quickly grew, and the event sold out within the first few days. Hosted at the Yale Club of New York City and attended by over two hundred people, this event has carried on since in various formats. Laura Donald was one of the women I invited to work with me and to speak, and I felt honored she chose to tell for the first time ever in front of strangers such an intimate story about her own journey to confidence.

Pregnancy has had the most impact on my journey growing a business. I forged these two new identities—mom and founder—at the same time, and they continue to intertwine. I decided to leave my last full-time job, being the breadwinner and very newly pregnant, to launch into independent consulting. Looking back on it, this was a pretty bold move, but it was the experience of trying to have a second child that changed everything.

Laura became pregnant a month before turning forty, when her son was almost two and her company was turning three. As an only child of divorced parents, she had idealized the nuclear family of four. Families with two parents and two kids seemed to her as more legitimate. As her pregnancy progressed uneventfully through the first trimester, she felt closer than ever to realizing her dream. She was preparing to travel for the holidays when she went in for a routine visit.

My doctor had the stethoscope on my belly. As we waited and watched, she played with the machine. We waited and watched some more. More playing with the machine, more prodding my belly. Nothing came to life on the screen—no sound, no motion. Then my doctor spoke my greatest fear: "I can't find the heartbeat." There was absolute stillness on the screen. I could see my fully formed baby girl with her elbow bent over her head. She will be frozen that way in my mind for all time.

What Laura described next was a blurry haze of events that involved a blitz of hospital activity, canceling most of her plans, and sharing devastating personal news nobody had prepared to hear. She clung to the doctor's comfort that her body knew best, and something must have been wrong. This termination was a compassionate way of ending a life that was not viable. She started that next year with the goal of healing and getting pregnant. She would get her perfect family of four before her son was too much older. All her energy went away from the healing her mind and body required and into what can only be called a fertility frenzy.

I'm not sure I've ever wanted anything as badly. I had made this desire for another baby about my worthiness as a woman. What is so clear to me now is it was about a lack of confidence, which I struggled with much of my adult life. My self-doubt didn't lessen as I became more accomplished or advanced in my career. Instead, I created this narrative about myself that my path, experiences, and choices weren't good enough. I was always minimizing myself and my journey compared to everyone around me to what I thought it should have been or could be. Even doing some pretty risky things, like getting a new business off the ground while newly pregnant, didn't shift my perspective of myself. I was courageous, and I still lacked confidence.

Laura had convinced herself that having a second child would make her family legitimate. After a long winter of trying, she conceived that April and started to feel more confident again. It was short-lived. A doctor's visit in May found her once again with a baby, but without a heartbeat. Reflecting on that time, Laura admits she took the frenzy to new heights by pursuing the most comprehensive IVF regimen possible.

By summer, I had my first appointment. By late fall, I was inject-
ing hormones into my glutes. The first round didn't work. Of all
our samples, only two survived long enough to be tested, and
none of those tested normal. I was not prepared for this result.
I thought our IVF plan of action was full throttle and, therefore,
airtight. Still determined, I stretched the bounds of what was
reasonable for us, especially financially, and went all in for a sec-
ond round. I knew the chances of it working were highly unlikely.
I knew, too, I had to find a way to be okay either way. I had to
let go of this idealized vision of how my family was supposed to
look. A few weeks later, I got a very surprising voicemail from
the specialist. We had one healthy embryo.

Laura's daughter, Olivia, turned five while I was writing this
book. While that beautiful outcome is heartwarming, it's not the
story. Laura certainly didn't think so either. This is not a lesson in
never giving up. It's about letting go of perfectionism as a path to
unleashing our confidence. No woman can control her fertility.
There's no *right way* to get pregnant. It's a process that teaches us
to let go, to accept ourselves and our bodies without judgment.
When we learn to do that, it opens up a world of acceptance for
other things beyond our control. Without the burden of comparison or the pressure of perfection weighing us down, we can
be confident. That's what Laura learned through her struggles.

Let go of however you think it's supposed to go or look or be.
There is only your own path, and it's just as legitimate as any-
one else's. It is not to be compared to or modeled after anyone
else's. It is to have its own unique quality and character and
unpredictable timeline. Confidence comes when you can let
go of what you think is supposed to be and embrace yourself
and your journey exactly as you are.

Axis Talent Partners celebrates its tenth anniversary in 2021, which means it will reach a milestone less than 25 percent of businesses ever do. While fewer than 4 percent of Black-owned businesses grow to have more than two full-time employees, they employ a staff of four, a crew of consultants, and boast annual revenue in the seven figures, which has doubled year after year since 2015. Laura has earned her bragging rights. Over the weeks we worked together to craft her story, Laura drew many conclusions, but it was only in a last-minute edit she decided on how she would wrap up her live remarks. She left us with these words:

Watching my business grow couldn't heal me, and neither did having my daughter and becoming a family of four. Becoming confident is ongoing work. But this idea helps: I don't have to walk any other path but my own. I don't have to look like, speak like, act like, or lead like anyone else. I get to be confident not because of something I've accomplished, but simply because I am being myself and nothing else. And you get to do the same.

BUILD AN IMPENETRABLE SHIELD OF SELF-BELIEF

"At the time, I didn't understand bias or racism at all. So I thought I had done something to make my teacher not believe in me, and I set out to show her she was wrong."

—DR. ROSHAWNNA NOVELLUS

There's an expression "game recognizes game," which means people can easily spot other people who play any game at the same level they do. They can see in another person if they bring the same standard of excellence, commitment, drive, follow-through, even finesse, and they respect them instantly, without ever having to say a word. The expression is a head nod to another in passing as you trade places on the court or any other arena. That's how I've always felt about Dr. Roshawnna Novellus, founder and CEO of EnrichHER. I could tell from the first time we met she plays to win. She was always impeccable with her word and her wardrobe. We became friends over the course of many events and casual meetups in Washington, DC during her time as a fellow for the social enterprise incubator Halcyon.

When someone is as confident as Roshawnna, onlookers sometimes get the wrong impression, thinking the road must have been easier for her than for them. Make no mistake, this woman is brilliant, but she's human and flawed like the rest of us and has had to construct an impenetrable force field of self-belief to counteract the many explicit attempts by others to talk her out of being great. It started earlier than one might imagine.

When I was in the third grade, my teacher pulled me out of class and said, "Shawn, I know you really love school, but you probably won't be very good in math because you don't have the capability." I was so confused because I did well in all my subjects, and I didn't understand how my teacher didn't know that. I didn't understand bias or racism at all, so I thought I had done something to make my teacher not believe in me, and I set out to show her she was wrong.

And prove her wrong she did. Roshawnna scored highest in her third-grade class in math and all her other subjects. By fifth grade, she was tutoring her classmates because she was so advanced. Yet her school refused to test her for the magnet program for talented and gifted students until her mother, herself an educator, insisted they test her daughter while she was present. Roshawnna tested off the charts, was admitted to the program, and was the valedictorian of every class from middle school through to her doctoral program. At every level, though, she faced unrelenting attacks designed to derail her and break her confidence.

Those early experiences in grade school taught me from a young age you didn't have to believe anything someone tells you just because they are older or have more authority. Even if you can't change their minds, you can change the facts, and by changing the facts, you change the narrative. I was the first Black valedictorian in the history of San Diego High School, the first high school in the city, and my GPA was the highest by a significant margin. But the administration was so opposed to letting me claim that achievement they tried to abolish the tradition of naming a valedictorian altogether. We had to get the local NAACP involved and threaten to sue them to let me give my speech.

When Roshawnna got to the University of California, Santa Cruz and majored in computer science, she led study groups with classmates. She consistently earned the highest grades in her classes while also tutoring other students, none of whom ever earned less than a B on an exam. One of her professors refused to believe she was achieving without cheating. He interviewed each of her classmates, even those outside the study group, to see if anyone would accuse her of cheating. He discovered no evidence of cheating. To his surprise, her peers credited her with rallying them all to achieve a higher standard of excellence. The professor apologized, but unfortunately, there were many other instances like this, and not all of them ended with humble acknowledgment of the wrongdoing.

Roshawnna learned to accept that not everyone will believe you, believe you are capable, deserving, and qualified. Her own belief in herself must always be strong enough to combat this reality. By keeping separate what she believes about herself from whatever anyone else imputes to her, Dr. Novellus can walk confidently into any room, take on any challenge, and persevere despite obstacles. It's all doable, but that doesn't make it easy. I asked her how she can keep her head up, especially now as a Black woman tech founder who hears "no" more than she hears "yes."

I have to admit, it's hard sometimes. That's why I focus on introspection, remembering who I am and what I've accomplished. Some have suggested keeping a running list of your awesomeness and journaling about your wins, no matter how big or small. Lots of people want us to fail. They would rather we fail than for them to have to reevaluate their biased practices and rigged systems. When we fail, it helps them justify the injustices. But once you realize people's intent may not be pure, you don't take what they say as truth, and that's liberating. Their words and opinions lose power over you.

We each need to find that place of deep belief in ourselves and go there in our minds and hearts whenever others use their words, their influence, or their resources to try and harm us.

"When I am facing a daunting task or unexpected trauma—the loss of a loved one, a job or title, the relocation of my family, or fears for my children's future—I remember there is little in front of me more difficult than the things I have already overcome. I reflect on the knowledge that when I am standing in and performing on my purpose, I can count on an inner flame of confidence."

—CLARISSA BEYAH

Just as confidence comes more easily to some people than others, it seems it also comes more easily at some points in our life than others. Clarissa Beyah is the founder and president of Writer's Block Ink, a nonprofit community arts organization that empowers youth as leaders using the power of spoken word through poetry, theater, and performance. She is also a chief communications officer and a full professor of professional practice at the University of Southern California. She tells the story of watching her own daughter grasp a microphone and start singing spontaneously at a family gathering when she was just seven years old. Amaiya, she said, stopped mid-song and commanded dozens of children and parents assembled around the room to rise, stand,

and sing with her. "And we all did. She transfixed the room with a magnetic power and presence, with confidence that penetrated and resonated."

Watching her youngest daughter often makes her wonder what fuels that flame of confidence so naturally, and when exactly it begins to shift and become overtaken by self-consciousness, anxiety, and fear. "What inevitable forces kick in and slowly erode it," she pondered aloud before adding, "and when do those flames of brilliance get doused with buckets of insecurities?"

It should come as no surprise Clarissa, an award-winning slam poet and an accomplished global communications executive, speaks in tantalizing sentences that drip with profundity and power. When I spoke with her about the role confidence has played in her success as a nonprofit founder and corporate leader, she offered insights on the phases of confidence in her own life and how overcoming the trauma of racism, abuse, and economic adversity has informed her mission of reaching the youth. For Clarissa, it started with what she calls *unconscious confidence*. Her retelling begins by revisiting her own experiences as a seven-year-old girl, which couldn't be further from Amaiya's experiences.

When I was seven, in my parents' efforts to protect us from the violence overtaking North Philly, they purchased a home on five acres in South Jersey. I started a new school. My former school in Philadelphia was an international Islamic community school with many first-generation African American Muslims and many immigrants from the Middle East. My new school was in the remote Pine Barrens of South Jersey

*in a tiny town known for fertile soil and small swamps—but
not for diversity.*

I entered that second-grade classroom, greeted by a sea of
white faces. I remember walking into the room, my hair
covered with a khimar, taking deep breaths, and having
no concept of the clouds of courage that softened each
footfall. When you grow accustomed to responding to
questions like, 'Why do you wear that thing on your head?'
unconscious confidence becomes ubiquitous. Up through
the ninth grade, I didn't think about the misconceptions
people have about what Muslim girls can, cannot, should,
or should not do. Thus, I didn't see religion as an imped-
iment to fully participating in life. I ran cross-country,
played basketball, was president of my freshman class, and
excelled in academics.

But in the tenth grade, when a fire destroyed our home, my
entire universe changed orbit. In the year that followed,
I'd go to three different high schools in two states, experience homelessness, rejection, religious ostracism, have my
innocence taken, and my confidence battered and molested
through the tumultuous process known as coming of age.

Clarissa credits unconscious confidence with helping her survive that period of time from age seven into her early twenties,
during which so much changed around her and within her.
Clarissa discovered a world of confidence through reading
and writing. Her escape into words and stories provide an
escape from the traumas she was experiencing. She found
purpose, something both bigger than and outside of herself,
to help her get through.

Writing saved my life. The warm and familiar walls and friv-olous competitions with my classmates to excel at honors and AP coursework enveloped and protected me. There was a world very different from my own awaiting me with the flip of a page whenever I needed an escape. From age sixteen to twenty-six, my life would become a collection of contrasts. I'd become a teenage bride and honor student, teen mom and team leader, slam poet, corporate executive, and university professor. As I climbed the corporate ladder in one world, transitioning from a low-walled cubicle to the corner office, I was also building another world, a small nonprofit for young people much like the displaced teen me.

The concept of the Writer's Block began in the cell blocks of incarcerated young people, all under the age of sixteen. Clarissa volunteered at a juvenile detention facility she passed on her daily commute on lunch breaks and in the evenings after work. Equipped with blank notepads, instrumental hip-hop beats, candy (sometimes, not always), and immense empathy, she helped her students discover they were strong and had a voice. Curiously, these young people, often illiterate by the standards of the schools that expelled them, were at the same time masters of their own rhythm and expression. Their words and stories kept her close to the writing and purpose that saved her life and served as a torch to light the path ahead as her changed circumstances put the trauma of her childhood into her rearview.

When I changed jobs, the new company didn't have a juvenile detention facility minutes away for me to spend my lunch breaks. My passion and purpose drew me to other creative adults looking to help at-risk youth. I teamed up with a collection of volunteers to help more than one hundred teens from several towns in southeastern Connecticut create a Black History Month production. I worked with the young poets. The production—which leveraged hip-hop to compare the racism and segregation of the 1950s to the present day—was a resounding sold-out success.

My small team of poets-turned-performers had written another play. When we couldn't secure support from others to put it on, two of those teens—who had infinite unconscious confidence of their own, Morgan Penn and Adriane Jefferson—inspired me to start a theater company. That was nearly twenty years ago. I became a founder at age twenty-six. Since that time, many of the young teens who participated in the Writer's Block grew into young adults and became staff members of the organization: writers, creative directors, dance, art, music instructors, and event producers.

Our current executive director, Juanita Wilbur, began as a Writer's Block student at age twelve, in 2007. Wilbur is the third consecutive executive director to join the Writer's Block as a young student and rise within the organization's leadership. The Block has served more than a thousand students and employed nearly one hundred young leaders. Nearly half of its board of directors are former students.

Clarissa has since moved beyond unconscious confidence, which she found through escape. Now she exudes what she calls "confidence on purpose." By leaning into her purpose, she feels confident in any setting, whether she's leading in a boardroom or speaking from the backdrop of a smart board.

Being "on" purpose for Clarissa means being intentional and doing what she believes has meaning in her life.

Writing saved my life, and in many ways, it's still coming to my rescue. Creativity powers my steps and compels me to cultivate atmospheres where those I have the privilege to lead can be seen, heard, accepted, and loved. I thrive on creating places that inspire authentic voices to own the microphone and the stage to tell stories that provoke social awareness and action. The moments in my life when fear consumed my confidence used to haunt me. Fear allowed me to allow others to harm me, diminish me, and make me doubt myself. I used to see those moments as sources of shame, but now I see them as fuel for my flame of confidence. When I am facing a daunting task or unexpected trauma—the loss of a loved one, a job or title, the relocation of my family, or fears for my children's future—I remember there is little in front of me more difficult than the things I have already overcome. I reflect on the knowledge that when I am standing in and performing on my purpose, I can count on an inner flame of confidence.

Laura, Roshawnna, and Clarissa's stories together helped me shed the weight of unrealistic expectations, insulate myself from the negative talk of naysayers, and draw my confidence from my own innate power. Recognizing the power of confidence, I wondered what would help girls and young women develop confidence much earlier and what it would look like for women to keep this confidence over time.

Kay and Shipman, authors of *The Confidence Code*, whom I mentioned at the onset, offer some hope for those of us who feel confidence may be beyond our grasp. It turns out we have

more control than we think. Although we may not be naturally or genetically disposed to show confidence, our brains'
retraining is possible, and we can become more confident
with practice. Habitual thinking affects our body and our
mind, creating new physical and neural pathways. So we can
choose confidence by focusing on the things that boost our
belief in ourselves by creating new habits and working on our
mindset. How reassuring to know that even if we don't pres-
ently feel like our most confident self, we can always grow.[8]

Armed with clarity and confidence, we're ready to explore
the next essential ingredient for daring: be creative.

---

8   Katty Kay and Claire Shipman, *The Confidence Gap* (New York: Harp-
     erCollins Publishers, 2014, 193).

CHAPTER 3:

BE CREATIVE

———

"The enemy of creativity . . . is fear. We're all born creative. It takes a little while to become afraid. A surprising insight: an enemy of fear is creativity. Acting in a creative way generates action, and action persuades the fear to lighten up."

—SETH GODIN

Social entrepreneurship, by definition, combines two things designed not to live together and fashions them into something new. It is the ultimate exercise of imagination to see enterprise as a vehicle for the betterment of society and not simply the enrichment of individuals. Creativity is vital to launching and sustaining a social enterprise. For women social entrepreneurs, having a healthy imagination is important because we are often trading in our current reality for a new one, for a better one that maybe only we can see, and this work must all start in our minds.

We truly are all born creative. If you've ever spent time around young children and placed a crayon or marker in their hand, they immediately go to work creating something. They don't stop to ask themselves, *"Who am I to draw? Am I an artist? How do I know what I make will be any good?"* Quite often, young children will drag the instrument along a page, carefree, and when satisfied, proudly show it off. It's a masterpiece in their eyes, whatever it even is. Many factors go to work on us to stifle, inhibit, and constrain that creative spirit. The little girl who sings, dances, and plays blissfully unaware of anyone's judgment or expectations in time learns to color within the lines, to confine her expression of creativity to the rules and external measures of acceptability.

For daring souls who want to make a difference, success often depends upon their ability to unlearn the rules and unburden themselves of expectations. Coloring inside society's lines may be safe but won't create change. It is often the intense desire to transform our circumstances and to escape discomfort that fuels our creativity. Faced with scarcity, loss, or grief, our desire to survive, overcome, and heal compels us to find a way through, and our imagination lets us see beyond.

Harnessing Your Imagination

It's approximately 6,022 miles (9,693 kilometers) between the capital cities of Warsaw, Poland, and Tegucigalpa, Honduras. Assuming one boarded a flight today from one of the major international airports in either country headed for the other, they would arrive about eighteen hours later and about fifteen hundred dollars poorer, accounting for the cost of air travel.

Now imagine you are a woman who has had to leave her husband behind in Poland. You have recently lived through the horrors of and survived the Holocaust and are seeking safety and a new life.

How would you feel denied entry into America from a ship full of refugees turned away at Ellis Island, and instead forced to board a banana boat destined for Honduras? What do you smell first as you make your way from the boat to a stranger's home and start the process of rebuilding yourself in a place where no one speaks your language and you must process the unspeakable atrocities of genocide? What soundtrack plays in your head as you are finally reunited with your husband two years later, and you welcome the first of your three daughters? When does this place become your home?

Those were some of my thoughts as I listened to Stephanie Nachemja-Bunton tell the story of being a girl who learned the necessity of belonging from parents who never quite enjoyed that privilege. Her mother was one of the three girls whose father established a tailoring business that put all of them through college in the United States, where they stayed two decades after starting from little more than skill, intellect, and dignity. Stephanie's dad was adopted, and he spent much of his life in search of a home, the kind that lives in the heart and not on a plot of land. This rich and relentless imagination Stephanie inherited drives her as cofounder of Meaningful Gigs. In this technology developer marketplace, world-class talent from across the African continent finds an opportunity, and their clients find brilliant translators to turn their design vision into tangible products.

Creativity in a very kind of direct sense has been super import-
ant throughout my life. As a kid, that was how I expressed
myself. To this day, I paint when things in general start to feel
challenging. It's my way of working through difficult emotions.
My favorite part of my job as an entrepreneur is creative prob-
lem-solving. We've had to do that a lot as a team. We have to
try and step into many peoples' shoes, understand what their
experiences moving through the world are, how they related
to our product, or how our product could make their life better.

Being an artist trains one to look at the same thing from
many angles, to step back and examine a different perspective, to be open to many interpretations, and this way of
seeing the world has given Stephanie an advantage in leading tech for a good start-up. As the only woman on a team
of three cofounders, she's learned to see her differences as
strengths, which help the team move closer to their goals.
Stephanie started her career in education working as a curriculum developer and instructional coach for DC Public
Schools, and later for a start-up nonprofit education organization. Her cofounders, Ronnie Kwesi Coleman and Max
Farago, had experience with technology companies prior to
teaming up in 2017 to launch the venture they initially called
ArtLab, and later pivoted to build a new company called
Meaningful Gigs.

The company name signals its commitment to leveraging
design for social change—first by making room in the global
gig economy for Black designers to be connected with projects that would impact and focus on job creation for a continent with the highest concentration of young people. In
the year since the shift, they have done well—matching over

fifty of Africa's best designers with jobs and putting them on track to bring over a million in revenue in their second year. Through all of this, Stephanie has kept a healthy imagination, even working with a mindset coach to help her grow her capacity for new and big things yet to come.

"I've sometimes wondered when communication feels difficult, 'Am I not being heard because I'm unclear or because I'm a woman?'" Stephanie has not been immune to any of the challenges. At times it hasn't been easy being the only woman on the team, especially since she brings such a different set of professional experiences to the table.

It's in these moments where I think about all the examples in my life of people who have had to carve out space, create an identity for themselves based on what they had that no one could take away. My grandfather had his education. He had his values of compassion, kindness, and humanity. I would think about how my mom had kept that alive for us. This company I knew was about helping people get an opportunity and be able to build a life using their skills, the way my grandfather did when he had to start over.

With intentional support and investment from Mayor Muriel Bowser and other municipal leaders, the ecosystem of support for women and new majority founders has grown considerably in the greater Washington, DC region. Reflecting on one networking event that featured successful female founders whose companies were earning as much as five hundred thousand dollars monthly revenue, Stephanie remembers feeling for maybe the first time like she had permission to imagine successful entrepreneurship in more human terms, that the prototype could, in fact, be someone like her. "Sometimes you just need to cry," the panelist had said. It was a simple insight, yet it felt like a relief to see expressing emotion not as a weakness but as a part of the process. It gave her permission to be more emotive and also encouraged her cofounders to honor emotion, to feel the highs and the lows, to embrace whatever they were feeling, and to be fully human.

When you are creating something that has never existed before, you are letting yourself be guiding by imagination rather than accepting what you see around you. It is natural for some fear to be present. In these moments, we may need to lean on the power of co-creators, our fellow disruptors, who are ready and willing to build with us if we let them.

UNLEASHING THE POWER OF CO-CREATION

"Creativity is a dance with fear and uncertainty, a journey into the unknown. There is a deep place within us that is untouched and whole. It is always present."

—NITA BAUM

When you have many points of connection and a number of overlapping relationships in common with another human, for some, it can become difficult to remember your first meeting—but not me. That's actually one of my weird superpowers. I have an uncanny ability to remember conversations verbatim, and I almost always remember the first time I meet someone. That I even got to meet Nita the evening we were introduced was a fortunate accident due to me running late for an afternoon coffee date with our mutual friend Kelli Doss.

That day, Amtrak was running behind schedule due to track work. (I've often wanted to know what it really means when the conductor says, "track work." It feels like a code for something. They always say it, but what are they even working on or doing?) I hopped on the 2 Train and made my way to the Financial District, and by the time I had a cell phone signal again, I could now read Kelli's text that she had dinner plans in Midtown Manhattan and wasn't sure we would have enough time to connect.

As I ascended the subway steps to ground level, trying not to get trampled by the impatient pushing of people who weren't climbing with a travel suitcase in tow, she started making her way to my stop. Kelli must have been doing mental math as she walked from the office to the train to figure out if I would be a welcome or disruptive addition to her dinner date with three friends, one of whom I knew because she was also a former colleague.

And therein was the problem. Kelli was in no mood to talk about work tonight. She wanted time with her ladies to have some wine and some laughs. As a chief people and equity officer for a rapidly expanding nonprofit organization, she talked and listened to people's discontents all day, and she was off the clock now. She didn't have much time to figure out what to do. Would my presence swing the dynamic of her evening toward polite work colleague chatter? Basically, would I cramp her style? Maybe. But it seemed she cared more about spending time together and was willing to take the chance.

Within a few seconds of spotting me, she said, "All right, Danielle, here's what we're going to do. You're coming with me. I've been wanting you to meet my friend Nita anyway." Excited and now very self-conscious, I realized my travel duds were not cute enough for the first impression I wanted to make. It was also too late to do anything about it. So I fell in step, walking with Kelli back in the direction I had just traveled, down the same steps, and back onto the train headed uptown.

We arrived at a swanky vegan restaurant, which I was told was Nita's pick "because she's been vegan for a minute, but we always make her go to restaurants that serve mostly meat, so it's only fair." We entered the dimly lit establishment to find three women whose skin was a rainbow of brown and whose smiles brightened as they saw us approach. Sitting dead center around the semi-circle fabric-upholstered bench was Nita. How we met may have been accidental, but that we met was purposeful. She has become a coach and a connector, helping me take the helm more boldly as the captain of my entrepreneurial voyage. As the founder of b*free, she has learned a lot about harnessing creativity to breathe life into ideas that become enterprises. As a woman who has built her companies while at the same time being a primary guardian and nurturer for two aging parents, whom she cared for until their passing, she understands the power of imagination and co-creation to help us endure dark periods.

Creation often begins in the dark. A seedling of pain or fear within makes itself heard. It signals change. It seeks attention. It calls for love. Part of my creative growth has been learning to turn toward, rather than away from, that seedling, which nourishes the fullness of our creative potential. My journey to b*free began in 2008. A seedling cried, "There is a misalignment between you and your work!" I left my job to create Alight. A freelance consultancy, we advised education-focused nonprofits, companies, and universities on strategy and organizational transformation. Alight prospered.

Working for myself opened a world of self-discovery, wellness, and creative self-expression. By mid-2012, our small team had completed a large-scale project we'd won in a bid against a top global consulting firm. Work and finances were thriving. We could keep riding the wave of success for the rest of the year or make room for a new direction. Earlier that year, I canceled a meeting of two hundred stakeholders. My mother broke her pelvis, a symptom of a deeper physical shift. My father was aging rapidly. Mom and Dad's changes awakened my own. Both life and death fuel creativity, reminding us there is only now. I spent the rest of 2012 in a creative process I call "curating my inspiration"—to reenvision, realign, and recreate my work to reflect on my identity and purpose.

Nita was born in Queens, New York, to parents who immigrated from India and came into their own as professionals and parents during America's twentieth-century civil rights era. She describes her father as a pharmacist, idealist, and free spirit whose heroes were Martin Luther King Jr., John F. Kennedy, and Gandhi. It was from him Nita learned to examine the human condition, to become curious about all the contexts in which an individual operated, not to judge but to understand them.

From grade school on, she was versed in liberation struggles and also grounded in the diversity of living in the most genetically diverse community in the world. Nita credits her mom, a pragmatic and gifted scientist, with helping her comprehend from an early age the relationship between what we consume and what we create. She wanted to create more vitality, longevity, and prosperity for herself in a world where she watched her parents lose their physical strength and slowly say goodbye to their material existence, and as she prepared her heart for the scarcity that grief would usher in by stealing away her beloveds. Nita didn't have the answers, but she did have an unwavering belief she could create a way through. She knew the answers would flow from inside out, which meant she could only take in the best things. So she started with her mental, emotional, and physical diet.

I experimented. If I align my consumption to my truths, will what I create reflect them? I studied the body, mind, and emotions. I traveled and meditated. I listened to music and talks, read and engaged in conversations and relationships that resonated with my soul. I exited habits and influences that didn't. I played, danced, and made music; 2012 was the beginning of a journey into myself, my roots, and embracing discomfort. It led to a powerful new integrity between my deeper truths and my contribution to the world. It birthed b*free. Projections *show that over half of the US labor force will freelance or be self-employed by 2027.*

We're at 36 percent today. What is the drive for this mass exodus from the workplace? What are we seeking? After studying and working with thousands, b*free's theory is we leave because the conditions of work do not nourish our wholeness. Often, the work itself is hurting the planet and all of us. People leave in search of meaning, purpose, and healing. They leave to create anew. What if the workplace was a healing space that saw you and created you as a whole? Our five b*free values emerged in response to that search:

We Are Free.
We Are Gifted.
We Are Equal.
We Are In Power.
We Are Grounded.

These values would be daily reminders to Nita of why it mattered not just that she started this company, but that she arrived at her destination. Until everyone in the freelancer and gig economy understood their value and could determine their own financial destiny, the value of their labor, and set the conditions for their work, they were not free. We all deserved to be, including traditional workers, but Nita would start her work with the people who were already taking steps to reclaim their power as producers in society. As she puts it, "b*free creates with a vision for individual, collective, and planetary freedom and sustainability. Our purpose is spiritual. Our vehicle is business. Our organization is community. If we come from wholeness, we will create wholeness."

Over the next three years, she would build from scratch a new way of being in a world when the people who gave her life were no longer here to provide reference points for her existence in it, and that would be the hardest thing she ever had to do. It would also only be possible because of the other constructive work happening inside herself and through her company. When she did a quick tally, she discovered she had coached nearly two hundred founders on how to launch their ventures for free in just a few years. She hadn't even noticed, not the time invested or the lack of compensation she demanded because she loved doing it.

Alignment would look like creating a business in an area where her energy was naturally flowing. According to a journal entry, she had that epiphany at 4:00 a.m. on January 9, 2013. The juxtaposition of b*free becoming stronger and taking shape with the decline of her parents' health was a theme that would emerge over and over in her self-reflections in the months ahead. By fall 2013, her mom was in a wheelchair, and her dad's seizures began. She had also hired a freelancer team, refined her business model, and started experimenting with new products and services. Within months, she moved her parents closer to her to care for them, and she engaged a team of home health aides and clinicians. She was managing the affairs for her home much like she managed her business—with heart and integrity. By early 2014, her dad was gone.

It was nonstop. My challenges illuminated where I felt small, disempowered, untrusting, afraid, and attached. It showed me the power of the village. And relationships, breath-work, and meditation reminded me what I forgot easily: how we build a thing is what it becomes. To become *a community, b*free had to be built by one. By December 2015, I hired fifteen amazing entrepreneurs to co-create our work. Working at the nexus of creativity, social impact, and business, my co-creators are diverse in gender, ethnicity, life experience, industry, and skills. We found each other through the resonance of our why. Co-creators are empathic, generous, and committed to self-development and truthful self-expression. I ask them to use b*free as a platform for expressing their highest motivations. Their growth and their businesses are integral to our mission, not a means but an end unto itself. We convened for a pilot gathering to launch our signature program for freelancers and entrepreneurs on Memorial Day weekend in 2016. Mom passed less than two weeks later.*

Sometimes I tease Nita. I tell her she should publish *The Book of Nita* because she has the most beautiful ways of phrasing things. She speaks in poems, permeating warmth and intensity that transfer like hugs over the phone. What I have learned from both her story and Stephanie is creativity is not just about making art. It's about making our lives more meaningful, more beautiful, and in the process, sharing the masterpiece that is our best work with others. For those of us who decide to create companies with the goal of changing the world, we must be equally committed to imaginative and constructive processes that will require rebuilding ourselves over and over in the face of challenges, losses, and setbacks. Yes, Nita, "We are each uniquely gifted. Discovering our gifts, strengths, and innate creativity helps us to awaken to, claim, and express our unique contribution to the world." We consider next how to find the courage to bring our gifts forward and contribute.

CHAPTER 4:

BE COURAGEOUS

———

"You learn to swim by swimming. You learn courage by couraging."

—BRENÉ BROWN

Starting your own company or organization is risky, but so is going to work every day for an employer at a company or organization you don't own and where you don't make final decisions about your livelihood. Everything we do in life carries some level of risk and also the possibility of certain rewards. My philosophy is that we reap the rewards not in proportion to the magnitude of risk that we take, but the frequency with which we take them. Said another way, we gain more in the long run by being intentional and habitual about taking calculated risks, putting ourselves out there, and seeing what happens than we do by taking sporadic big risks without a plan.

Maybe it's the emergence of entrepreneurship as a lifestyle and the proliferation of said lifestyle through social media that has led to the growth some of us call the "hustle porn" industry. Ubiquitous, toxic, and addictive, with the barrage of messaging urging people to work harder, sleep only when they're dead, and succeed by any means (or die trying), it's no wonder more and more people who take the leap of entrepreneurship are falling into unhealthy patterns, battling depression, and even taking their own lives.

It takes courage to define success on one's own terms, to go against the popular discourse and the real and perceived external pressures. We need courage to break free from the expectations of even well-meaning family and friends who might encourage us to take a *safer* route. We need courage to keep looking deep within ourselves and trusting our gut, even before there is any real proof we are on the right track. But what is courage? Where does it come from? How can we get more of it?

Pop quiz: How long do you think it would take to do a quick scan of all three hundred million mentions generated by Google search for the word *courage* (assuming you spent only one minute per page?) Five hundred and seventy years. Courage is a popular theme, and for good reason. It is essential to human existence, and yet we aren't born with it. We cannot even be certain we have it until tested. It can increase or decrease with time. It can surprise us by dissipating when we most need it or showing up at unexpected moments.

I define courage as doing and facing anything that makes me afraid or doing something despite feeling fear, which is close to the textbook definition. To show valor, boldness, or bravery on the outside, we first need courage, which is a quality we develop deep within. We can show courage even when we aren't confident we'll succeed. It's the willingness to try, to fail, to live with the consequences, come what may, that makes us courageous.

The courage I'm interested in, the kind I believe every social entrepreneur must embody, is the sort Brené Brown mentioned in a Facebook post on February 14, 2019.

"The root of the word courage is cor—the Latin word for heart. In one of its earliest forms, the word courage had a very different definition than it does today. Courage originally meant 'to speak one's mind by telling all one's heart.' Over time, this definition has changed, and today, courage is more synonymous with being heroic. Heroics is important, and we certainly need heroes, but I think we've lost touch with the idea that speaking honestly and openly about who we are, about what we're feeling, and about our experiences (good and bad) is the definition of courage."[9]

It's not surprising she would share this definition on a holiday when many people grapple with matters of the heart, but the resonance of courage defined this way extends far beyond anything superficial or performative. At the core, courage is speaking our truth. Our path to being courageous requires we first get comfortable in the discomfort of our own truth, especially when being true to ourselves puts us in conflict with others.

---

9   Melissa Kiss, "Courage—A Matter of the Heart," *Thrive Global*, March 29, 2018.

SITTING WITH THE DISCOMFORT OF OUR TRUTH

Sometimes we buy into a myth unknowingly. What happens when facing the truth is uncomfortable? Will we have the courage to speak up, making room for beliefs and a new narrative? For Melissa Campbell Brogden, founder of Campbell Impact—a boutique fundraising strategy firm that supports nonprofits—and the self-proclaimed "human Swiss Army knife," the road to being courageous started by rejecting narratives that no longer served her. For starters, she had to let go of the fallacy. She was an exception, something she had believed throughout her academic career and even as a young professional.

The truth is I got dealt a good hand even though I grew up in poverty. I always had good choices. I had a parent who didn't work full-time and could go to every parent-teacher conference, who could be a real present figure in my life, and who had a network of relationships that she knew how to leverage for my good. I never saw myself as having deficits. In fact, when you're a scholarship recipient all your life, always gaining access to highly selective schools and programs, you get used to the performance of poverty and appreciation to your benefactors. You start to buy into the idea you're exceptional, and that's why you deserve what you've received. I performed exceptionalism better than most, and I felt very confident in spaces where I received praise and attention for being what others expected me to be.

Melissa attended elite schools all her life, including Spelman College and the University of Pennsylvania's Graduate School of Education, where we met. She's brilliant and driven, and all of her talent and hard work landed her in leading nonprofit, policy, and philanthropic organizations over the course of her career. Being a foundation grantmaker and later a nonprofit fundraiser forced her to confront a fallacy she had believed from her youth and into adulthood: some people succeed and deserve opportunity because they are exceptional.

No longer a recipient of charitable gifts, she was on the other end of the relationship. Watching organizations with the best of intentions perpetuate the dangerous idea that some poor people were exceptions and more deserving of being invested in and supported than others made her uncomfortable. She had believed for too long she could prove her value to others by how much she accomplished, by excelling. Now, she could see the weight of these expectations for what they were— another subtle form of racism and classism.

Admitting this to herself demanded courage. It meant she had to acknowledge a different story than the one she had been telling. It required courage to call attention to the fact the beliefs upon which her profession built ignored under-lying issues of structural inequality, which often benefited the wealthy and kept some people and neighborhoods poor. Cherry-picking the exceptions would never lead to long-term transformation.

To place the onus of escaping from the oppression of poverty on the shoulders of the children and youth from low-income families is to shirk all responsibility for the systems that have disadvantaged them and the people who designed and upheld those systems. In this new light, she found it untenable to keep up the pretense of being the overachiever who could do it all. Being a "human swiss army knife" meant constantly striving to live up to unrealistic expectations. She was no longer interested in perpetuating the myth.

Melissa decided to champion a different and more sustainable approach to reinvesting in people through redirecting philanthropic giving and also by means of her community investment as a property manager who rents homes in neighborhoods with great schools to working-class families with the support of government subsidies, all to help give them a leg up in academic and financial attainment. She hopes to change the conversation.

It became clear to me we had to stop investing in the farce of exceptionalism. Then maybe we could push nonprofits and mission-driven organizations to truly deliver on their promises because then we would remove the misguided idea that poverty is a choice. In reality, it is not about helping one person at a time escape because they worked hard enough or even saving people. It's about sharing resources and supporting people to build all the capital they need to create their own solutions.

Melissa's desire to leverage the fullness of her lived and educational experiences led her to launch her own firm, and as a founder, she faces challenges that test her courage. It is often a balancing act between protecting her business interests and her brand while also taking a stand for things that impact her and her community.

These days, I spend a lot of time thinking about how to position myself as an activist and spokesperson for the issues important to me. As a Black female entrepreneur living in the South, I'm affected by racial and social justice issues, but I also know I have to protect my business because I don't have a safety net. There's a real risk for people who are self-employed or just starting up to play nice and not be too disruptive.

There is no one way to be courageous. Although we have divergent worldviews, I could relate to Melissa's challenges. Often, my views are misunderstood and maligned since I am politically neutral. Still, the courage it takes to speak up is never wasted. It is always worth it, even when it's not easy. I asked what she has learned that might be useful to other women walking this tightrope of courage. Her advice is to look for alignment over agreement. There are times when we may not agree with potential clients, but we may still have areas of alignment. By not insisting that you agree with everyone you work with on everything, you may find ways to keep growing your business without giving up too much of yourself.

What I spend my energy pursuing is alignment. Are we moving in the same direction? Alignment doesn't mean you agree with my thoughts, share my perspective, or believe in the mission the way that I do. My only requirement is that you don't get in my way as I pursue my vision. As long as I can do what I need to get done and you're not obstructing that, we can figure out a way to work together.

It is one thing to face your truth and quite another thing to be self-determined in living it out loud. Sometimes we hold back from speaking our truth because we don't want to disappoint others or lose out on opportunities.

SPEAKING YOUR TRUTH WHEN IT MIGHT COST YOU

My own story of learning courage through practice starts with an interview for a job I thought I needed and thankfully didn't get.

She was a lean woman with a bright smile, voluminous, cascading red hair, and the most intense brown eyes. By this point in the selection process, I had been reminded over and over, by the recruiters, by my interviewers, by the application itself, how challenging it would be to teach in an under-resourced rural or urban community. I had gone to school in one such community, and the kids I was being told to fear, both because they wouldn't measure up and also because I might not, were younger versions of the kids I grew up with and me. These kids were my cousins, family friends, and neighbors who were still in school. These kids were infinitely capable, just as I had been at their age, just as so many of my former classmates were, and they needed teachers who believed in them, not people who pitied them. When I sat down across from this young woman, who couldn't have been more than a few years older than me, I was struck by how formal she was and how foreign everything she described sounded.

As I listened carefully to my interviewer discuss her experience teaching in the Mississippi Delta, how different life there was for her, how little she had known about the region before arriving, and how much she learned while she was there, I found myself struck by the descriptors she used. Words like "eye-opening" and "transformational" stood out. My mind trailed off a bit to how I had gotten here. The interview process had many steps, including screening conversations, a panel interview where the applicant taught a mock lesson and was graded, and then a final interview with an alumna. I was starting to feel the pressure to get a job as graduation approached, so here I was at essentially the last step in the process.

It's one thing to be a daring girl or teenager. When you have bold, creative ideas and pursue them as a young person, people tend to be impressed. You are called a trailblazer, natural leader, go-getter. Everyone expects you to grow up to be and do something important, as long as it's not too risky. Lots of well-meaning adults in my life tried to steer me toward what they considered safer career options. No one ever even suggested I should become an entrepreneur, despite my showing an early aptitude for leadership, enterprise, and problem-solving.

In 1984, the year I was born, the idea someone could be a *social entrepreneur* was still under debate. It seemed oxymoronic. Until then, altruism was the domain of charity, not business. That same year Bill Drayton, who coined the phrase and then campaigned for its adoption in the decades to follow, was elected a MacArthur Fellow. This appointment validated both the term and his vision for how the world would shift as people began to see themselves as changemakers.

Drayton hypothesized that if anyone with an idea had the agency to create new organizations to better society, then we could accelerate the pace at which we solved problems. No more waiting on governments or idealistic philanthropists to get around to fixing things, community actors would drive change and collectively shift the way systems worked. With the prize funding he received, he devoted himself full-time to the organization he started just three years prior called Ashoka.

According to David Bornstein, the journalist and historian who chronicled Mr. Drayton's journey and the evolution of the field of social entrepreneurship in his book *How to Change the World: Social Entrepreneurs and the Power of New Ideas*, it took another two decades for his ideas to reach a tipping point. As I was growing up, so was the field I would later enter. None of this happened by accident. Drayton had intimate knowledge of how change happened within systems at the intersection of business, government, and society. He had learned to foster the conditions under which his seedling idea could become a forest.

Over twenty years and many shoutouts from presidents and global leaders later, Drayton's efforts paid off. Social entrepreneurship had its *"Mama, I made it"* moment around the turn of the twenty-first century when business schools and institutions of higher education began creating pathways and programs for credentialing people who wished to apply entrepreneurial methods and advance new models for social and economic development. Wendy Kopp, founder and CEO of Teach for America, was, not surprisingly, an Ashoka Fellow.[10]

Near my college graduation, anyone who didn't fit into the more prescribed paths leading to a career in medicine, law, or finance moved toward the social impact. Nonprofit careers were certainly not new, but the sector was undergoing a

---

10   David Bornstein, *How to Change the World: Social Entrepreneurs and the Power of New Ideas* (New York: Oxford University Press, 2007, 48–59).

full-blown renovation as new players entered and created companies designed to bring the best and brightest talent into good social careers. In retrospect, it's easy to see how and why mission-driven work appealed to millennial sensibilities. Many factors converged.

My peers and I started our careers during a financial recession. Where our parents' and grandparents' generations had to be won over to a new way of thinking about the role and responsibility of business, we needed little convincing. For millennials, this is what we've always known: there was a better, more sustainable, more socially conscious way to operate. We were also impatient about career advancement and about the pace of change. With the emergence of technology companies and venture capitalism, we witnessed some of our classmates drop out of college to start companies and raise staggering amounts of money. This was also creating another generation of younger, savvier funders convinced we could *hack* any social problem using the tenants of traditional enterprise.

My parents, who had encouraged me to dream out loud, who had nurtured my ambitions, who had supported all of my daring pursuits (remember the eight-year-old who planned a retirement party), now seemed to be getting nervous as the final semester of college arrived. I still hadn't landed a full-time job. Most of my friends were interviewing with management consulting firms, investment banks, or taking entrance exams for medical, business, and law school. None of those paths felt right. I wanted to take some time away from school to gain real-world experience before I committed to anything else, and my heart was pulling me in a more entrepreneurial direction.

Over my four-year tenure, I had worked in six different non-profit organizations. The education I received from local community leaders, policymakers, and the community foundation representatives felt more resonant to me than many of my courses. To my parents' dismay, my grades sometimes slipped, and always for the same reason. I had taken on robust extracurricular activities. Leading multi-campus events for the Black Student Alliance at Yale, helping a friend to grow the audience ad broker sponsorships for *Sphere*, the college's first print and digital magazine, and serving as a student board member for Dwight Hall at Yale (the community-service-focused nonprofit housed within the college) were just some of the activities that helped me hone the professional skills I use even now.

As adulthood beckoned, something else was calling too—student loans. Being the first person in my family to attend such a pricey college meant being the first ever to take on the debt that came with it. My parents and other well-meaning adults in my life were looking out for me, pushing me to be responsible and get a job—a good-paying one. I resolved if I must get a job, it would be working with and for the people who were daring, the ones who were following their dreams and doing good in the process. That's what landed me in this interview, sitting across from a woman whose eyes seemed to search through me.

The interview was going well until we broached the topic that was a dealbreaker on both sides. Would I be willing to go wherever they placed me? Something in me knew to say yes if I was going to have any shot. This was the last step in a long interview process. I could call my parents and let them know

I had a job, and I would be okay. But I simply couldn't. I told the truth.

Teach for America was opening a chapter in Connecticut, which was why I decided to apply. This was my home, and if I was going to make a difference for Black and Brown kids, I wanted to do it at home where I felt a real connection to the community and where I felt I would be most impactful. I was not interested in serving in rural America, and I would not accept a placement if it meant being anywhere I wasn't excited to teach.

As I expected, her smile flattened to a line, and I could see in her eyes a certain disappointment. Then it sunk in. Her truth was different from mine. Her reasons for signing up for this were different from my own. It didn't seem worthwhile to try and convince her, and there wouldn't have been enough time. The interview ended politely, just as it had begun. I knew I would not be getting the job. Misty-eyed, I called my mom on my walk home. Sparing her no details, I told her the exact moment when I lost the job. She tried to cheer me up. A few days later, an email confirmed what I already knew.

What felt like rejection was one of the most helpful redirections of my life. A few weeks before graduation, I received a service fellowship from Dwight Hall at Yale, the on-campus community service organization, and got a placement for the summer at a local nonprofit. It felt good to have something lined up. It felt even better to have some time to explore my options. By the fall, I landed a job in a start-up education policy organization where I was the first communications manager and only the fifth hire. That job changed everything.

There I got to pursue my passion for creating education and economic opportunity, serve my home community, and discover my knack for elevating human stories.

All this became possible because I was courageous enough to speak my truth, knowing it would close a door, not knowing if or when another would open. As a rule, whenever I have the option of speaking my truth or saying what others want to hear, I always choose to be courageous. By giving myself permission at the start of my career, I learned the consequences of being true to myself weren't so bad. My theory is that if we edit ourselves out of fear, we will erase opportunities by telling the truth when, in reality, all we erase is ourselves. The clear lines that make up who we are become blurred and obscured until we disappear. No wonder by the time we are five, ten, twenty years into our careers, we have lost sight of who we are.

Fast forward about ten years. I found myself sitting across from the same woman who interviewed me as a college senior. Her face was unmistakable—same smile, same hair, same eyes. This time she was hiring for a job I absolutely wanted, leading marketing and strategic communications for a growing college success organization called iMentor. Everything had come full circle. Not only did I get the job, but it was also one of the most defining moves in my career. That opportunity put me on track to make another significant leap and launch my company. Katie, the woman whose values seemed so misaligned from my own just a decade earlier, became my champion as a supervisor, a trusted friend, and one of my first clients. All this resulted from being courageous when I had no way of knowing how things would turn out.

I'm convinced the world either contracts or expands in proportion to the room we create for ourselves in it. Each day we are faced with the choice to etch our stories permanently into history or to erase the lines with which we draw our humanity.

LISTENING TO THE COURAGEOUS VOICE WITHIN

There's a famous quote often attributed to Nelson Mandela, which states, "Courage is not the absence of fear, but the triumph over it." One of his contemporary namesakes is a bold and brilliant woman named Mandela SH Dixon. As the fearless leader of the global accelerator for diverse tech start-up founders, Founder Gym, she often tells entrepreneurs in her community to "Do it scared." Do what? Do anything that's important to growing your businesses, anything that really matters to you, even when you are afraid.

Our introduction came from Nicole Jarbo, a super-connector, fundraiser, podcaster, founder of a fundraising consulting agency called Goodbets, and most recently, Boost, and a tech start-up that aims to disrupt jobhunting for GenZ. It feels like a privilege to be in the same orbit. There are few people whom I've felt as connected to, despite never having met face to face. Nicole and I launched our companies around the same time, and we have hundreds of overlapping professional relationships. I have learned from her how to be stealth, steady, and strategic. Goodbets is in a strong place, and she can see a clear path to grow her revenues to over one million dollars in the next year. Getting here took effort, patience, and discipline. At times, it took a toll on her health. She knows what many people would advise her to do, what seems like the safe bet. But her heart is in Boost, the start-up she's self-funded with bootstrapped capital.

Nicole credits her friend and business coach, Mandela, as one of the people who has challenged her to think bigger about what's possible. This isn't surprising. Hearing Mandel's story inspired me to listen more deeply within and trust my gut too. Listening to her speak, whether during a virtual training or an in-person dinner, you get the sense her pep talk is as much a reminder to herself to keep her own flame burning as it is meant to ignite one in her listeners. It wasn't easy for Mandela to be courageous when faced with the choice between what seemed to be the ostensible right path and the path that was right for her, and maybe that's why she has so much conviction.

Mandela says she found her community and her calling when she attended her first hackathon and won. She describes it as a lightbulb moment that interrupted her entire way of thinking about what was possible for her life. Until then, she had identified as an athlete, as a teacher, as a compassionate problem-solver, but never an entrepreneur. One education-themed hackathon opened her eyes to a world she never knew existed, a world where anyone with a great idea could find other people willing to work on their idea and fund it.[11]

I don't want to say I was cowardly, but I wasn't standing firm in what I knew I really wanted. This is a lesson I've learned

---

11   Lisa Nicole Bell (host), "Mandela SH Dixon on Reinventing Herself and Flipping Failure into Success," Behind the Brilliance, April 4, 2019.

*over the years to listen to my intuition more, and it's taken
me a while honestly to develop this skill.*

Not yet ready to go all-in for her new passion, she pursued
her doctorate in education by day and worked on her start-up,
an education technology company, by night. Listening to her
inner voice, the one that was trying to get her attention from
the moment she won that competition, helped her determine
which ball to let drop. Graduate school could wait indefinitely,
but not her entrepreneurial dreams. The voice warning her to
stay on the more established path, to do what would be better
for her career at the time, to avoid the unnecessary financial
risks, was really just fear talking. Listening to those voices
would have kept her playing small. Her advice to founders
who are similarly conflicted is simple:

*If you can't stop thinking about it or dreaming about it, if it
gives you more joy than anything you've ever experienced, this
is your life telling you something.*[12]

Our truth will not stop calling out to us simply because we
ignore it. To be courageous, we must sit in the discomfort of
our truth. To be courageous, we must speak our truth even
when it could cost us. To be courageous, we must listen to the
voice within that calls out to us, even when it's inconvenient
or scary. How far we go, and how quickly, will be determined
by whether or not we choose courage over fear.

Nicole and I have a way of going months with no contact
but then catching up over long chats. It never feels forced

---

12   Ibid.

or awkward. Toward the end of 2020, we scheduled a quick thirty-minute video call that turned into a three-hour conversation. It was one of the highlights of my year, and given that I had just completed this manuscript, it felt good that so many themes I touched on were resonant. She is exactly the person for whom I wrote this book. She reflected on some of the milestones she achieved amid a pandemic, some of which she didn't even believe possible just two or three years ago when the world felt more normal. She said, "I'm not dreaming big enough. I know that now, and I am ready to stop playing small."

It was so relatable. Nicole is all of us at some point. She does not lack confidence in her ability. She knows she is smart, scrappy, and that she will be successful at anything she gives energy. But she has learned how to play safe, and now she's ready to play big. Brené Brown says, "You learn to swim by swimming. You learn courage by couraging." In daring, there is no substitute for doing. If you've ever taken a big risk, you realize at some point that no matter what happens, it's rarely as grave as whatever apocalyptic scenarios you played out in your head. You were quite likely surprised that things turned out even better than you could have expected. Being courageous will sometimes stretch us to our limit, but it will always be worth it.

We've covered a lot of ground. As we consider the fifth and final daring habit—build community—you'll notice a shift. Whereas the first four rules help us do the internal work that prepares us to stand boldly in our truth, persist despite challenges, and believe in ourselves, this next and final rule is all about how we show up with and for others.

In building community, our goal is to establish winning relationships that will go the distance. Networking takes time and energy. How do we build community across lines of difference, in ways that are generous, genuine, and generative? Are there any time-saving hacks for growing our network? How can we make more meaningful and memorable connections? All that and more can be found in the next chapter.

CHAPTER 5:

BUILD COMMUNITY

---

*"Yes, I needed a lot of miracles! And they came
in the form of other people, showing up at
the right moment, in the right way. Mentors,
cofounders, investors, customers ... We
made me the success that I am today."*

—TIFFANY NORWOOD

Founding a venture can be a lonely endeavor, even when
you're succeeding by all objective measures. One cannot
overstate the importance of building community. A great way
to start is by engaging with the people who are your peers,
those who are building alongside you, and those who are a
bit farther ahead of you and still proximate enough to really
understand what you're going through. It can be tempting
to want to network with more successful and accomplished
entrepreneurs. Some founders spend a lot of time and money
attending dinners, conferences, and events, joining exclusive
groups and social networks, all to get an audience with the

people who appear to be the upper echelon in business and investor spaces. While it is true that social networks matter in how entrepreneurs gain access to capital, garner warm introductions to potential backers, and establish credibility, that's not nearly the whole picture.

Meeting Angel Rich was years in the making, though it didn't happen until 2017. After graduating from Hampton University in 2009, she started her career as an analyst for an insurance company based just outside Hartford, Connecticut, which is about a thirty-minute drive from where I grew up. During the same years Angel was saving Prudential billions of dollars as a rising star in their annuities division, I was spending long days helping to shape education policy at the state capital building only a few miles away from her office.

Unbeknownst to me, Angel was working on a financial literacy solution for the same populations of kids and families for whom I was advocating for expanded educational access. We had many shared connections but were unaware of each other. A few years later, I moved to Washington, DC. By the time I launched my company and got involved in the tech and social innovation start-up scene, Angel had achieved a record-breaking number of downloads for her app, WealthyLife. She had also written a best-selling book called *The History of the Black Dollar*, been famously dubbed "the next Steve Jobs" by *Forbes*, and was a recent appointee as commissioner to the DC mayor's Financial Literacy Council.[13]

---

13   Geri Stengel, "A Black Women Entrepreneur Only Gets Funding Crumbs," *Forbes*. May 3, 2017.

We ran into each other several times over the course of many months, and each time Angel was quick to give of her time and advice, and always with a smile and a funny quip. She was one of the most memorable and highly rated speakers at PurpleCON, the annual convening my company hosts for social enterprise and tech for good start-ups. She shared her path to scaling a tech start-up as a woman and founder of color with humor and honesty that shifted the energy in the room. Even more noteworthy, when she arrived at the conference, she wasn't alone. Unbeknownst to me, Angel invited her mentors, two powerful women entrepreneurs, one of whom became a trusted advisor and coach.

Why mention this? Angel understood the power of community. She opened her network to me without my even having to ask. Sometime later, she mentioned that leading up to the conference, she had been thinking about how she could best support me. While she could not purchase a paid sponsorship, she realized socializing my event with influential women would be better than money. Her thoughtfulness touched me, and she was right. Make no mistake, it was expensive to produce a full-scale conference. Every sponsorship dollar mattered. At the same time, I understood that investment comes in many forms. I've always been incredibly fortunate to have people in my life who believed in me and became the miracles I needed to pull off impossible things. This hasn't been an accident. Relationships are capital, and they can be converted like any other currency when managed properly.

But how do we build community? Let's review strategies and stories from other women who have been successful in finding their tribe. A word of caution: if you're anything like me, you may have some baggage to release. Networking can be exhausting and depleting, and when we put ourselves out there, there is always the risk we may get burned. Here is where remembering that daring is not a single event but rather an ongoing cycle of doing, asking, receiving, and embracing, which helps us stay committed to the process. It may also require defining more loosely what it means to create value and extract value in relationships. It's possible some of our community will be people we never meet in person. The goal is to spot opportunities for meaningful connection and develop more powerful ways of engaging.

With all that said, we're ready to explore perspectives on how to build community in a way that's authentic and accelerating. Here are some of the things I've learned from personal experience or picked up watching others.

NEVER UNDERESTIMATE THE POWER OF PERSONAL TOUCH

Thanks to public relations mogul and author Terrie M. Williams, I learned early in my career the art and science of a well-written note. Reading her book, *The Personal Touch: What You Really Need to Succeed in Today's Fast-Paced Business World,* was like getting a crash-course in the etiquette of business networking. On more than one occasion, I had the pleasure of hearing Ms. Williams speak on the power of genuine connection and gratitude, among other topics like Black trauma, healing, and mental health, at live events.

It wasn't until 2016, when we sat next to each other for the last leg of our Amtrak ride headed to New York City, that I was finally able to thank her personally for how her book and good advice helped me in navigating my early career. Two things I learned from her was to do your homework before reaching out to someone and to always express gratitude to anyone who gives you their time, ideally with a hand-written note. I can't say I'm always perfect in this regard, but I've consistently found ways to personalize my outreach.

Given our hyper-connectivity across social media and the abundance of ways to gain intel and access to other humans, there's no excuse for not knowing about someone before reaching out to them. This is an incredible advantage when crafting cold emails, which will not just get read but will garner a response. In the first three years of building my company, I sent hundreds of cold emails and LinkedIn messages to various individuals I thought would find value in partnering with me. What I've learned is most people want to be helpful to others, but they need a reason to stop whatever else they're doing and take action. It's up to you to make a case for them, to make it easy for them to get to yes. If you can't show them why it's the best use of their time to support you, you haven't done your job. Make it personal. Align your ask to the other person's interest. Consider bringing a small gift to your first meeting to introduce yourself, like branded swag or a gift card for coffee. It's really the thought that counts.

Dozens of my professional relationships started with cold outreach and blossomed into strong partnerships because they were watered with gratitude and built from an alignment around shared values. Zach Wade, the former CEO of MakeOffices, responded to a cold email and offered me five months of free coworking space after learning more about my start-up. Kurt Slanaker, former director of House DC at Eaton in Washington, and Noga Tal, global head of partnerships at Microsoft for Start-ups, agreed to meet with me after I sent them cold messages on LinkedIn and outlined how their programs would benefit from being part of my conference. Not only did they sign on as lead sponsors, but they also galvanized support among their colleagues to ensure my event was promoted and well-attended. We are still in touch, and despite living on different continents and time zones, I am always astounded by how seamless our communication feels.

Never underestimate the power of the personal touch. I'm not advocating for being stalkerish or presumptuous. In fact, doing your homework should help you narrow your outreach to individuals to whom you can add real value and with whom you believe there will be alignment around shared values. Before you send that first email or make that cold call, do a quick scan. Your message shouldn't be all about you and what you want. It should be about the person on the receiving end.

THROW YOUR OWN PARTY AND YOU'LL ALWAYS BE INVITED

A mistake many people make as they build community is expending an inordinate amount of time just trying to get in front of the right people. They worry about getting invited to events, invited to speak, and invited to pitch. What I have found to be the better investment of time and energy is to build something worthwhile to attract people to you. Nobody wants to miss out on a great party, so throw the one everyone else will want to attend.

I'm not suggesting we all should plan events. Whatever you're doing, whether it's your YouTube channel, podcast, or an online community you curate, that's your party. Your goal is to amplify solutions to problems and improve the lives of real people, to create value through the experiences others have with you. When you're creating value, this will make you magnetic to the right people, and your profile will grow. You won't have to chase anyone down, at least not anyone who matters. By focusing on throwing your own party and building your own brand, you will be less distracted by what others are doing, less tempted to waste your time and energy reaching out to people who may not even be the right people with whom you need to connect.

By age twenty-seven, Tiffany Norwood had done something few, if any, other entrepreneurs have since, which is to raise $670 million to fund a start-up—the world's first-ever global digital radio platform, which launched three satellites in space. Now on her seventh start-up and counting, Tiffany codified the methodology that led to her success. It has at its core an uncompromising belief in the power of the collective, the power of we. Tribetan, the science of turning imagination into reality, is a venture designed to help people take their dreams seriously and then find the tribe of people who are out there waiting to help. Lots of emerging entrepreneurs, and even seasoned ones, would love to be mentored by her, but she's very selective about with whom she works. Tiffany was one of the women that Angel Rich personally invited to attend PurpleCON. What she saw that day impressed and inspired her, and it was the reason she was open and ready to partner with me when I reached back out.

In summer 2020, at a time when my imagination felt stymied, it was a joy to be invited into an intimate circle of fellows who are all handpicked by Tiffany to be coached and mentored for a year. My sister-fellow is Lolade Siyonbola, the Afropolitan founder of NOIR Labs, a global creative and multimedia company that curates content and connections to celebrate and elevate Black excellence. Whenever I am in the virtual company of these women, I think about how this is only possible because I took my own ideas seriously, even before I had the support from others to realize them. By being brave enough to throw my own party and not wait to be invited, I could attract amazing people.

You can do the same, and I encourage you to start by thinking about ways you can invite other people into your work. Consider hosting virtual or in-person coworking days with other entrepreneurs where you informally share where you're getting stuck and where you're finding success. Have you thought about starting a new tradition, maybe a brunch meet-up a few times a year for other women entrepreneurs you admire but don't know very well? When AdeOla Fadumiye, whose company Crys & Tiana helps entrepreneurs launch podcasts and increase their brand visibility, invited me to a private brunch with five other founders in our region, I had no idea what to expect. The warmth and generosity of those few hours, though, was exactly what I needed, and the connections I made that morning led to future referrals.

GO BEYOND TRANSACTIONAL EXCHANGES TO FORM TRANSFORMATIONAL RELATIONSHIPS

Who is someone to whom you are loyal? Your hairstylist, gynecologist, therapist? If so, why? It's probably not because they are the only option in town. Most likely, it's because this person has been there for you in transformational ways. Maybe they pushed you to try a new hairstyle and you received lots of compliments, which boosted your confidence. Maybe they were with you through a health scare or major life event. Not everyone we engage with will have such an intimate story, but the point remains that transformational relationships are stickier than transactional ones. Do you remember the name of the gas station attendant who sold you a pack of gum or the cashier who rang you out at the grocery store two weeks ago? Maybe not. But what if I asked you who was the friendliest cashier with whom you've ever interacted? You may never forget that person. We build community by looking beyond what we need at the moment and thinking about how we might exchange value in the long-term.

We may need to check our expectations about what someone can offer us. Many people who have successfully built enterprises and who are ten, twenty, even thirty years ahead simply cannot relate to the context in which entrepreneurs are building and navigating today. They may not understand all of the technology that powers your digital marketing scheme or be able to help you fine-tune your customer acquisition strategy, but they will be able to share other timeless nuggets of information. Possibly, they will be able to help you improve your executive presence, your negotiation, your emotional intelligence, or your mindset.

It will always be a winning strategy to treat advising conversations like a buffet rather than a three-course meal. In other words, see everything served to you as an array of options from which to choose. Carefully inspect and select what you take away from the spread instead of simply eating everything put in front of you, regardless of how well-plated. Another thing worth saying, not everyone needs to understand every aspect of our experience to be part of our community. There is room for all kinds of supporters on your team. Some will be mentors, sponsors, advisors, and investors who can help champion you and your venture, and they may come to the table for different reasons. Superficially, they may not share much in common with you. What matters is you can discover the shared values connecting you and work from there.

Something I've learned from the Tribetan Method is to trust the transformational power of community, which is to see the abundance of wealth that exists just by our connection to others. All we have to do is turn to our neighbors, open our hearts and our hands, and the generosity we show will attract more of the same.

Kristen Coffield and I shouldn't be friends, but we are. We are at different stages in our lives, and we couldn't possibly show up more differently in the world. I'm a Black millennial woman with Caribbean family roots, dark curly brown hair, and Hershey chocolate skin. When we met, I was still a newlywed and starting my business. Kristen is an attractive blonde-haired, blue-eyed woman in her sixties, with the physique and stamina of a woman in her twenties. A serial entrepreneur for over the past three decades, she has successfully raised three children and stayed happily married, all while beating throat cancer, caring for aging parents, and weathering financial setbacks that nearly bankrupted her family. Another big difference, she's a morning person. A regular contributor to *Good Morning Washington*, Kristen is often on TV sharing health and nutrition tips.

Somehow, Kristen and I ended up seated next to each other three times in a row at networking meetups hosted by Elle-vate Network. These were mostly transactional networking opportunities where women came looking to drum up new business or talk about their services to get referrals. But after the third time of politely exchanging pleasantries, Kristen and I decided to meet for coffee and get to know each other better. As founder and CEO of The Culinary Cure, Kristen helps people use food as medicine and fuel, allowing them to level up in every other part of their lives. She has compiled thousands of recipes and health hacks, many of which are available for free on her website; others can be found in her book *How Healthy People Eat: An Eater's Guide to Healthy Habits.*

Kristen knew she had a powerful story and message and was looking for help to think strategically about how to keep growing her brand presence. She couldn't do it alone. In the process of starting my business, I was neglecting my health, not eating well or exercising enough, and it was creating a bad cycle I found hard to interrupt. How serendipitous we kept finding our way to each other, not realizing we had something the other was seeking. Within a short time, we discovered many ways to be mutually supportive. This wasn't a transactional relationship. It was about helping each other transform how we were doing business and level up.

We are connected to each other in so many ways now it's easy to forget we started as total strangers. Our friendship represents one of the more transformational relationships I've forged since starting my business. Kristen introduced me to DeDee Cai, founder and CEO of Fit to Profit, who became my wellness coach and whose encouragement helped give me the push to capture my story and write this book. Every event I've planned in the greater Washington, DC area since 2017, Kristen has been part of as a caterer, speaker, and mostly as a friend and cheerleader.

People enter our lives at different seasons and for different reasons. If we're paying attention, we'll notice where there is an opportunity to plant a seed that may later blossom. It also helps not to write anyone off simply because they are different. They may surprise you.

LEVERAGE THE POWER OF YOUR AUTHENTIC STORY

Our goal isn't to attract everyone. A key to building community is attracting *your* people. I love how Gbenga Ogunjimi puts it in his book *Borderless Voice: The Power of Telling Your Story and Defining Your Identity*:

When you tell your story, you activate your 'tribe.' Your tribe is a community of like-minded individuals who share common interests and values. It is within this tribe where miracles happen. It has always been there, waiting for you to come into yourself and find your true voice.[14]

It's imperative to lead with your story to connect with the right people at the right moments to accelerate your venture. This means letting people see the real you from the start, not a facade. When we lead with our story, we make

---

14 Gbenga Ogunjimi, *Borderless Voice: The Power of Telling Your Story and Defining Your Identity* (Self-published, 2018).

meaningful and memorable connections aligning with our values. It requires more upfront preparation and reflection to be ready to show up in our full humanity when we meet new people and as we build relationships.

One cannot overstate the power of storytelling. Humans have neurological wiring allowing them to engage with stories. This is just one thing that separates us from animals. I like to say that storytelling is the only way we know how to communicate ideas in a way the head and heart understand simultaneously, and people with far more expertise in brain science agree. Wanting to better understand what's going on in our minds when we are hearing or telling stories, I asked my friend Dr. Jos'lyn Woodard, a neurosurgeon, to break it down for me. The first thing to know is that stories engage the transmitters in our brain that trigger our emotional responses and impact our decisions. Here's her full explanation:

No matter how much we want to intellectualize and rationalize our decision-making, quite often, we are driven by emotion. Many people have heard of brain chemicals like dopamine, which fuels our reward pathways, and oxytocin, which fuels our attachment pathways. Both of these neurotransmitters are activated when you become engrossed in the stories of another because there's an emotion that becomes activated by the storyline and because you've formed a personal attachment to the character.

We also learn and retain information better when it's conveyed to us in narrative form because it stimulates and connects activity in the part of the brain where we decipher language and store memories. Dr. Woodard continues:

Most people get bored listening to fact-based lectures. Pro-cessing information doesn't as readily trigger the connection between the frontal and temporal cortex of the brain, which is associated with language comprehension and memory encoding.

All of this shows that what happens in our brains when engaged with a story is complex. There's no one part of our brain that is activated but, in fact, multiple areas. Liz Neeley is the founder of Liminal Creations, a design firm specializing in blending the art of storytelling with the science of research. Prior to that, she was the executive director for The Story Collider. This nonprofit organization curated live and digital storytelling experiences where real people told science-based stories to spark learning and innovation. Over the course of her career, she's helped scientists, researchers, and everyday people tap into what she calls the "delicious feeling of being swept into a story world" for the purpose of advancing scientific knowledge and changing human behavior. So it may be hard to believe there was a time when she was skeptical about whether story-telling was more than just a distraction to real science. In an interview with Maddie Sofia for *Short Wave*, an NPR podcast, she confessed her misgivings:

I wanted to be the most serious, scientific scientist who ever lived. I thought storytelling was somewhere between a dis-traction and a danger. I thought storytelling was what you did when your data was weak in order to sort of nudge people toward your preferred interpretation.[15]

---

15   Sofia Maddie (host), "Your Brain on Storytelling," Short Wave, Janu-ary 14, 2020.

What won her over was seeing in action, over and over, the power of storytelling to help change how people engaged with information, took inspiration from it, and, ultimately, changed their beliefs and actions. Now she's partnering across the scientific community to make this standard practice. Like Liz, many of us know we should lead with our story to make more meaningful and memorable connections, but we get stuck. Maybe we don't feel like we're particularly good at telling stories. Others feel like they are inauthentic or gimmicky when they engage with narratives rather than just state the facts. For others, it's about fear of being misunderstood, judged, or exposed. We may reason that if we are too vulnerable, we open ourselves up to criticism. These fears are not unfounded. What could help is to reframe the fear as an opportunity.

Rather than fixate on what could be lost by showing up more authentically, by connecting on a more human level, maybe consider what you have to gain. You will have an advantage over the many people who still resort to inundating others with lots of information they don't care about or even remember. You will attract the people who are most excited about what you're creating, and you'll energize and activate them to support you. Finally, you will weed out the people who don't honor your full humanity and save valuable time and energy as a result.

Something Dr. Novellus said in her interview stayed with me and feels instructive on the point of how to build a community.

Most people in this world won't see the amazing, beautiful, capable being inside of you. Don't expect them to, and remember they don't matter. The people who do are your allies, supporters, and customers. They see the real you, they believe you, and when you focus on them, you worry less about all the others.

Your people are looking for you, and you can make yourself easier to find if you lead with your story.

STRETCH BEYOND YOUR COMFORT ZONE

In our digital world, community isn't just the people we see face-to-face or interact with every day. We have the capacity to reimagine our networks as concentric circles with varying degrees of intimacy and interconnection. During the process of writing this book, I've interviewed dozens of women, gotten input from dozens of other authors, and consumed hundreds of talks, podcasts, articles, and social media posts. Not everyone in our community will be part of our inner circle, and that's as it should be. Every person whose expertise I've sought along the way is part of my community. Their voices, their stories, and their lessons are now part of my own.

A helpful rule of thumb is to look to well-established business leaders and entrepreneurs for inspiration, and not much more. Said more bluntly, don't be a clout chaser. Instead, try to focus on building your circle from the inside out. Rather than going big and broad, start small and deep. Sometimes we prefer to talk to strangers about our ideas because we feel like the people who know us best may not understand or may judge us. This can be uncomfortable, and you know best what energy you need around you. You could start by thinking about people you often see at events or in your network. Maybe schedule an informal meetup. You may get more curious about what your own friends are doing, who they know, what they are interested in, and look for ways to support them.

The people most proximate to you today will be the ones everyone is looking up to and trying to get access to tomorrow. My advice is to invest in your future by connecting with them now. On more than one occasion, I've seen the power of horizontal networking pay off. My peers have invited me to co-create content and experiences with them, supported my events, hired me, and recommended me for consulting engagements. Many of the voices included are women in my network whose companies are doing amazing things and who motivate me. My hope is you will see them now as part of your tribe, as the people you can look to for insight and inspiration.

We may not realize we're in a bubble, so it's good to mix things up. Lara Holliday took a road trip that changed her life. Miles away from her regimented schedule, bustling family life, and Brooklyn brownstone, she was totally out of her element in rural South Carolina when it occurred to her she had been living in a bubble, and she did something about it.

It was the fall of 2015, and I was intently looking forward to the possibility of seeing a woman break the final glass ceiling. I signed up as a campaign volunteer and a few weeks later found myself driving through what is known as the heir lands on the outskirts of Charleston, South Carolina. This area is populated by folks who are direct descendants of the enslaved people forced to work the land for no compensation. Being there helped me realize how detached I was day-to-day from the realities of so many others' lives. I found a new appreciation for community, and I returned to New York City committed to expanding my community beyond my intimate circle of friends.

We may not always be able to take time away for such a long road trip, and some of us may find we have opportunities in our everyday lives to pause and engage with greater intention with the people right around us. But for Lara, even living in one of the most racially and ethnically diverse cities in the world, she still found her life had become too homogenous. She saw no challenge to take on the worldview of others with different socioeconomic backgrounds.

After that road trip, which was then followed by several more, I settled back into my life in Brooklyn and got right to work. My desire to facilitate and leverage the power of community led me to launch Tide Risers, a global community where women grow together as people and professionals. We have locations in seven cities, and we come from all walks of life. I've learned that when we find what unites us, we can draw upon that commonality for strength and support. We are stronger, braver, and more fulfilled within our networks when that community helps to push us past our comfort zones.

We can't and shouldn't all start our own new networking groups. There are plenty of amazing formal and informal communities of support for women and women of color, some of which I've mentioned, like Tide Risers, Ellevate Network, The Cru, Black Girl Ventures, The Melanin Collective, Hello Alice, IFundWomen, and EnrichHER. What we can and should all do is be more intentional about how we show up and connect.

We've discussed quite a lot in this chapter, and it all comes down to this: there is no such thing as a self-made entrepreneur. Building community is necessary, and the most enriching relationships will be the transformational ones based on shared values that push us out of our comfort zone. Even if you don't know exactly how to help or support the people in your life who are building and scaling a social enterprise, you will never go wrong by opening your network up to them. It can be as simple as sharing their content, liking, commenting, and tagging them on social media, or sending a thoughtful note of introduction on their behalf. Finally, don't be afraid to show up and lead with your story. Let people see the real you, and know you are enough, the right people will appear to help you when you need it most, and generosity attracts more generosity.

We've come to the end of this section, and now you know how to "Dare to Think Purple:"

Be Clear
Be Confident
Be Creative
Be Courageous
Build Community

But along the way, we all discovered nuggets of wisdom we wish we knew sooner. In the next section, we'll discuss seven of these themes that came up over and over in my conversations with mission-driven women entrepreneurs. I call them the *cheat codes*.

HOW TO DARE: DO, ASK, RECEIVE, EMBRACE

Eduardo Placer is a classically trained professional actor and a renowned international public speaking coach. Founder of Fearless Communicators and a self-proclaimed "story doula," he has supported women and men across the globe in standing more confidently in their bodies and elevating their voices, speaking with the intent to be heard, not simply to make words with their mouths. He is also a generous collaborator, who graciously agreed to offer feedback on my opening remarks for my conference in 2019.

Call it Murphy's Law, but on the day and time of our scheduled coaching session, everything seemed to be going wrong. I had to take the call on speakerphone in my car shuttling from a vendor pick-up. We made the best of it. Eduardo listened to me rattle off my talking points, and then he left me with four words that conveyed what should be my challenge to the audience: Do, Ask, Receive, and Embrace.

Why pause to share this anecdote? Because Eduardo will forever be woven into the fabric of my own storytelling, and because he is a reminder to me, and I hope to all of you, that no one is an island. I have been made better, constantly, by the creative people who help me see myself and the world more clearly and walk more confidently through it—the people who challenge me every day to keep daring. That speech turned into a framework that I now use with my clients, and which I'm passing along to you. This is how to DARE.

Do.

This can mean to perform a task to work on something. When I say that DARE-ing must start with *doing*, I mean that to make anything important possible, you must be in active pursuit. I mean *do* the way I believe Nike means it when they say "Just do it." That *do* stands in for whatever action gets you to your goal, helps you focus and achieve, pushes you beyond your perceived limits, and ultimately, results in victory.

Think back to the eight-year-old girl you met who was donning her pink sneakers, her Lisa Frank rainbow-colored accessories, and was making her way into the school building and headed straight for the principal's office, not knowing what the answer would be. That's how active pursuit looks. It's taking the first step, and the one after that, and the one after that, getting in motion and staying in motion, with no guarantee of success.

Do: Get in motion; stay in active pursuit.

Ask.

The fear of being judged for what we don't know or can't do often leads us to hold back from asking for help. The more we make it a practice to ask, the easier it becomes. Imagine that little girl later mustering the courage to pull her art teacher to the side after class and share her plans for the party, chatting the idea up with a few friends at lunchtime to get them excited, and sharing the news with her parents to get their support. There was no way for a third grader to pull off an idea like this without asking for help.

Kids are naturally humble and unashamed to admit what they don't know. Have you ever noticed how people coax and encourage a baby to learn to say their first words? Compare that with how some people treat adults learning to speak a new language, sometimes their third or fourth. Somehow, people can be more patient with baby babble than with a heavy accent. It's that judgment we often hope to avoid, but we can't let it stop us.

Daring requires investment and support from others, and since other people can't read our minds, we have to ask for what we need. There are a bajillion proverbs about asking, and the same ideas show up in almost every culture. "If you want to go fast, go alone; if you want to go far, go together." "The squeaky wheel gets the oil." If you want to build a social enterprise and change the world, ask for the help you need. With everything stacked against us, why make it harder on ourselves?

ASK: Request help from others; don't try to do it alone.

Receive.
Have you ever stalled so long getting back to someone it was almost too embarrassing to follow up? Maybe you were at a networking event and they gave you their business card or connected with you on LinkedIn, and all you had to do was respond and set up a time to chat. But you didn't. Or maybe you feel super defensive, sensitive, or protective of everything you're working on,

so you put off getting feedback from anyone until it's perfect. Only it never seems perfect enough, so days, weeks, months, years pass and you're still in the same spot.

If any of that sounds like you, then you may need to learn how to receive. It's not enough to ask for help if we aren't ready to take in what others have to give. This doesn't mean every critique, suggestion, or idea will be valuable. But we won't know if we aren't open in the first place. Quite often, when we don't receive, it is because we don't feel worthy enough. Other times, we have taught ourselves not to depend on anyone else as protection against disappointment. We may have valid reasons to keep our defenses up. Ultimately, though, receiving starts in our minds. If we cultivate a positive and abundant mindset, we will more readily open ourselves up with the belief that good is coming to us, and we will be ready to receive it.

RECEIVE: Accept help when it comes and resist the urge to overthink.

Embrace.

Not everything goes as planned. Even when we are actively doing, asking for the help we need, and receiving support from others, there will be surprises, detours, and setbacks. Sometimes we execute our plan and celebrate success at the end. Other times we get to the end and all we have left are some purple lanyards (yes, I'm still a little bit salty). Regardless of what happens, we always win when we embrace the lessons learned and apply them the next time around. It's appropriate to grieve a loss for a period of time, but then it's time to get back in motion. Daring is a daily endeavor. There is no graduation from daring. No one will award you a medal. It's a mindset and a practice that you perfect through perpetual use.

Embrace: Learn and grow, whatever the result and without judgment.

THE CHEAT CODES

It's great to know the rules, but sometimes it's even more important to know the "cheat codes." These are the hacks that can help save you time and get you to your destination faster. Here are seven that I hope you will find valuable.

CHAPTER 6:

ACKNOWLEDGE THE PLAYING FIELD IS UNEVEN

———

"The start-up industry is based on gaslighting and gatekeeping. Nearly all of the successful tech founders have a few things in common: they are rich, well-connected white men. And that's all they had to be."

—BEA ARTHUR

Let's assume the very best-case scenario. It might look something like this: While growing up, you learned to believe girls are infinitely capable, smart, and strong. You had great role models and an enormous amount of love and support all your life. You were born into generational wealth, attended the top universities in the world, and graduated with no college debt. Later with your savings, you were able to self-fund your start-up. You are mentally, emotionally, and physically well, able-bodied, and identify with the majority culture. You feel accepted, safe, and like you belong where you live. Your partner shares all the work in your home evenly, and you had no trouble when you were ready to start having babies. As a mom, you enjoy the perfect mix of child-rearing support and family support, which allows you to balance the demands of work and parenthood without stress. You sleep eight hours each night, plan your meals and workouts just right, and make time for quiet reflection and journaling to start each day. Sexism, bias, imposter syndrome, and self-doubt are not issues in your life.

Does that sound like any woman you've ever met? Nope. Everything is way too perfect. The problem is every item in that scenario points to the challenges faced by most women we know. Women entrepreneurs are dealing with all of that plus all the stuff that is germane to all founders. If we normalize being honest about the reality of building a social enterprise as a woman, then we can be better prepared to turn any challenges into steppingstones instead of roadblocks. We aren't making it up, and by *it*, I mean the significant barriers women must overcome that our male peers never even have to consider. By naming this, not just quietly among friends but out loud and in mixed company, we interrupt the shame and end the gaslighting that interrupts progress. Only then can we start being more intentional about how we build, how we partner, and how we survive the start-up process.

Recognizing that being born a girl and growing into womanhood means enduring a unique set of biological, psychological, societal, and sometimes cultural burdens in no way diminishes or undermines how powerful women are. It also does not disinvite men from being true allies and collaborators with us as we win at hard things. It's about telling the whole truth and making room for the stories too many of us hide or downplay, fearing others will perceive us as weak, unqualified, or petty.

Where I had premonitions about what makes the playing field uneven for women, the experts I interviewed had science and facts to validate these hunches. A few themes emerged from my conversations with Krystal Morrison, clinician and PhD candidate at the University of Central Florida, and Bea Arthur, a licensed counselor turned tech entrepreneur whose company, The Difference, is making mental health services accessible to everyone through on-demand therapy. Next, I examine just three psychological and social realities making the entrepreneurial journey harder for women.

WOMEN ARE GIRLS WHO GREW UP WITH SOCIETY'S UNREALISTIC EXPECTATIONS

Young children form their identities, expectations, and aspirations based on the adults in their lives. In time, their peer relationships and society also exert a significant influence, but a lot of early wiring forms the basis for how we see ourselves in the world. When there are simply not enough examples to draw from to broaden our beliefs about who and what we can become, this can take time and intentional work to shift.

Krystal Morrison and I have been connected for over a decade by dear friends and family, but I only recently learned of all she's been doing as a clinician to support individuals who are healing from childhood trauma and coping with post-traumatic stress disorder (PTSD) and other anxiety disorders. When we connected, she was in the final year of her doctoral program in psychology, which means that by the time this book is published, it will be more accurate to call her Dr. Morrison. We discussed current knowledge about the socialization of girls in their early years and why having access to role models early in life can be determinant of who they become as adults.

We are all a product of not just our psychology, which is our own interpretation and perception of the world, but also of our socialization, which involves the way the world interacts with us. In early childhood, our world is smaller, and we learn through our caregivers, our family members, our peers, possibly a religious community and extended family members, and then school. It expands as we get older. As children, we learn the expectations placed on us and which roles we will occupy later in life. Early on, we observe who does the caregiving, chores, good manners, and we receive early cues about sexuality. Quite often, the expectations fall unevenly for girls and boys.

This reminded me of what Tara Mohr describes in her book, *Playing Big: Practical Wisdom for Women Who Want to Speak Up, Create, and Lead,* as the "good girl conditioning" so many of us receive very early in life. As she explains, "Be nice. Be considerate of others. Don't rock the boat. Be likable. Be modest and solicitous at all costs. Don't ever be angry, aggressive, or arrogant. In the context of this conditioning, the withdrawal of others' praise or their negative reactions to us feel particularly transgressive and scary."[16]

---

16   Tara Mohr, *Playing Big: Find Your Voice, Your Mission, Your Message* (New York: Avery, 2015).

This goes beyond what my mom always called "good home training." I certainly am not advocating for teaching girls to be mean, inconsiderate, abrasive, immodest, and prideful. Being in the company of misbehaving children grates on my nerves, and I don't enjoy being around grown people who lack home training, either. Being kind, thoughtful, respectful, humble, and generally displaying good manners are basic things to instill in children, and not just little girls. That's the point. Girls are too often taught to be agreeable and are subject to character assassination if they are anything else, while boys often get a pass.

Being the first of her parents' children born in the United States after the family immigrated from Ghana, leaving behind a comfortable life to give their children more opportunities, Bea Arthur felt the weight of *good girl training* intensely as a youth. On some level, she understood why her parents set such a high bar. They had given up so much to start over in a country where they felt disrespected and ostracized, and they worked hard. Not only did they not ask anything of their children they weren't themselves doing, but they also weren't asking Bea for more than she could do. Bea was special.

Her talent and gifts were apparent from a young age, which led to her being sorted into the most challenging academic programs, being accepted into a highly selective magnet school, and being signaled out for her achievements. She admits, like so many high-achieving girls, she liked the accolades and the attention that came with performing, and she started pushing herself. It all became self-reinforcing, only it wasn't sustainable.

Once puberty hit, everything in her world changed. Her body transformed, her hormones seemed to take control, and she had no vocabulary for expressing all that was going on. Bea describes a rush of new feelings and thoughts, including suicidal ones. There seemed to be no space for all this conflict in her parents' imagination or the expectations of her teachers. She was still a gifted, high-performing student, and by all measures, a good student, but no longer a good girl. It was all devastating, but it set her on a path toward healing and understanding.

Through her therapy practice and as a health tech entrepreneur, she answers what feels like the calling in her life to ensure everyone has access to mental health services. Always at the top of her mind is her younger self and the adolescent girls who are going through all the challenges she went through. Retraining herself, setting aside the need to live up to impossible expectations, has given her the mental toughness to navigate the tech start-up world.

Good girl conditioning is especially powerful for children of immigrants in America, and the expectations just keep building. We are taught to obey, to behave, to perform, and not to complain. Girls are trained to seek approval and praise, and if you don't disengage from that as a woman starting your own business, it will be to your detriment, especially if you are a heart-led founder, because you feel personally connected and responsible for the change you're hoping to create.

When we have ultimate accountability for decision-making and when other peoples' livelihoods and economic interests depend upon us, this only amplifies people-pleasing instincts.

We want to do a good job, and it can feel like failure is not an option.

Things go wrong all the time, and you literally won't be able to function if you need constant praise and approval. If you don't check the praise expectations, you come undone. Investors don't want to hear any bad news, and you can't tell your employees bad news because you have to keep morale high. Even when you try to share with your friends when things aren't going well, they don't really want to hear it either. The amount of work that goes into these short-lived rewards, the highlight reel everyone else sees, is unfathomable.

While it could be tempting to take a hard stance on what is good and bad, Krystal suggests it's helpful to avoid these categorizations and to instead seek to understand every belief and behavior in its context. If we look at why women developed certain tendencies and why parents may have felt it necessary to raise girls with certain expectations, it was often in response to external forces that limited their power and self-expression or a desire to protect them, to enable them to navigate more safely.

Oftentimes, what we learn represents generations upon generations of practices, and we should ask not whether they are good or bad, but adaptive or maladaptive. What we need to understand is whether or not our habits are serving us now. There are contexts where some of these taught behaviors in these roles and gender expectations could be helpful. But then when you grow into womanhood, and you are pursuing a career in sectors not heavily occupied by women and where the ways you're socialized aren't welcome or valued, then it may be good to reevaluate some of the things you've learned and come adept.

Bea suggests there's a golden window for parents with daughters between the ages of ten and fifteen to intervene in a powerful way and help shape the next generation of girls to become women who understand the power of their voice and trust their instincts. Rather than place the full weight of our expectations on girls and young women, it's important to help them think about who they want to become and how they want to use their voice, and to help them develop and use their internal compass rather than looking to other people—be it their peers or their parents—for validation. If we want to make the road smoother for women in the future, it starts by adjusting how we raise girls today.

WOMEN'S LABOR IS LARGELY UNSEEN AND UNDERVALUED

Society expects women and girls to do more, even in the midst of a pandemic, at least within the home. UN Women reported on the disparate impact of the COVID-19 pandemic on women and men, stating this crisis "underscores society's reliance on women both on the front line and at home, while simultaneously exposing structural inequalities across every sphere, from health to the economy, security to social protection." They found even when things are relatively stable, women, on average, do three times the amount of unpaid work in homes as compared to men. With children out of school and many more people getting sick, it's women who are more likely to have their schedules interrupted, including their business operations, to take care of their families.[17]

---

17 UN Women, *Policy Brief: The Impact of COVID-19 on Women*, New York, 2020, accessed October 29, 2020.

Even though she leads a team that specializes in helping companies do right by working parents, especially moms, Callan Blount Fleming is not immune to how these insidious inequities show up. She empathizes with women who struggle with giving themselves permission to make room for their businesses while managing their responsibilities on the home front. When faced with the dilemma of who should give up working to take care of the kids, she says society's unequal compensation and underinvestment along gender lines often make the decision a bit too easy. "When women in hetero relationships sit down with their partners and do the math, and she's making only eighty cents to his dollar (if she's white and even less if she's Black or Latinx or disabled), it seems like a no-brainer for her career to take a backseat to his. And that's just it. Until we invest in women's companies and pay women equally, we'll never solve this problem." It's worth mentioning that as of 2017 (the last year of available data), two in five American heads of households are women who are the sole breadwinner. For women of color, the ratio is even higher.

It could be easy to miss all the ways men have been disadvantaged by a system that demands so much less from them, even as it affords them a series of undeniable advantages. That, however, would be a mistake. Just as a muscle shrinks when it doesn't get much use, we shrink in our capacity to be fully human when we're not exercising all the dimensions of our humanity. Said another way, because society hasn't asked men to be more than providers, procreators, and sometimes physical protectors, many men are underdeveloped in all the other facets of themselves. Just as girls learn to participate in the reinforcement of profoundly unreasonable expectations, boys learn their reductive, prescribed roles, which are also detrimental. They learn to perform machismo instead of masculinity. On this point too, Bea offered really fascinating insights.

Men aren't winning in this system either. They have experienced a boost because of an invisible economy of women, the female economy beneath them, holding them up. As a result, they learned to be providers and procreators, and since that's all they have, they become competitive with other men and don't develop the other relational skills. Focusing only on those things, basing their identity on just those things, has led to a selfishness and simpleness we see too often in dominant male culture. When that is our example of leadership, it's sad.

It seems to come down to choosing a new paradigm of leadership, modeled more closely to the values and characteristics a vast majority of people prefer. Everyone benefits when we demand more of men and women, and it starts with how we socialize boys and girls.

Women rise to the occasion because of the high expectation placed on us. We have learned to be caring, to handle complexity. We can manage when things get complicated. We can handle our feelings and others. We shouldn't be trying to create the next Mark Zuckerberg, Elon Musk, or Jeff Bezos. We should be teaching you to be whatever is the new model for the CEO that involves using power in ways that are compassionate and human and healthy. Imagine if we required boys to explore and develop their emotional intelligence the way we require girls. Just think about how companies would look and run.

Ultimately, this is not about asking boys and girls to occupy the same roles. It's about expanding the scope of the complementary roles men and women play in our family, community, and society. It's about acknowledging when we ask less of men and boys, we hurt them as much as we do the women and girls who must then pick up the slack and whose labor goes unseen, unvalued, and uncompensated.

It's worth stating another benefit of reimagining masculinity is we normalize uniquely feminine ways of leading, relating, and creating. Maybe if we expand our definitions, women could finally be compensated for their labor at an equitable rate. Maybe the pay gap could close in our lifetime instead of in another 250 years or more. Maybe when women stood on stage to pitch, they could do so without having to second-guess if they should have taken off their wedding ring to avoid questions about how they will manage all the unpaid work expected of them by their husbands and kids while also building a company.

This is all conjecture, but the fact it's all based on reality is why the first cheat code for surviving the first five years in social entrepreneurship is to acknowledge things aren't the same for men and women.

SOME WOMEN HAVE IT EVEN HARDER THAN OTHER WOMEN

There are levels to this inequality game, and yet there's no winning for anyone. Without looking at where gender intersects with race, ethnicity, ability, and under-marginalized identities, we won't get a full picture. Cheyenne E. Batista is the founder and CEO of Firefly Worldwide Inc., an organization whose mission is to support mission-driven leaders to achieve excellence with intentionality in a collective push for a more equitable world. As a doctoral candidate at American University concentrating in education policy and leadership, she is on a mission to transform instructional systems, practices, and academic leadership in public schools. Cheyenne has thought a lot about how all of her identities have made her experience different from many of her peers. While she notes there are challenges, she chooses to frame her differences in terms of what advantages her perspective affords her.

For every degree of the margins you live in, for every layer of the margins you live in, it doubles the perspective you bring to any context and, therefore, doubles your ability to problem-solve, doubles your ability to innovate. By nature of being a woman, being a Black woman, being a Black Latina, being a Black Latina who is a first-generation college student, grad student, now doctoral student, now business owner, all of those sorts of firsts, and all of those ways in which I've had to navigate systems not designed for me means I have to be that much more aware compared to whoever is sitting next to me. I have to be much more aware of the many complex realities around me.

Melanie Rivera is a mission-driven intrapreneur and entrepreneur. As the partner for educational equity at The Management Center, one of the leading training and consulting clearinghouses for social impact managers, and as the founder and chief executive officer of Breaker28, a boutique coaching practice for high-performing leaders, she helps nonprofit executives break through the barriers to achieving equity and excellence in their organizations. What I find most impressive about Melanie is her openness toward collaboration and mutual learning.

Though we have yet to meet in-person, we have connected for Zoom meetups. Melanie has quite literally written a book's worth of content tools and case studies on the importance of addressing intersectional, or overlapping, identities when we think about how to remove the barriers to entry and success for people who get overlooked.

I asked her thoughts on what makes entrepreneurship more difficult for women of color, and not surprisingly, she had a lot to offer.

My own life experience has shown what makes this so much more difficult for women of color, and it has a lot to do with expectations. The same things that might make you a really good employee, like the ability to keep your head down and work, work, work, are the same thing that can make you a really bad entrepreneur and CEO. People want something different from the founder of the top executive leader than they want from a worker bee. They want authenticity.

According to Melanie, this is as much brain science as common-sense, but it can be jarring when the rules of career advancement change and suddenly there is an expectation of leaders to be more authentically themselves when conformity is what made them successful in the first place.

We are bioengineered not to trust people who appear false. Women who haven't been asked to be themselves, and, in fact, have been asked to edit or hide or suppress their self-expression to fit into the mold of their organizations, often are given the feedback that they are closed off when they get to the C-suite, and they don't know what to do. To get people to invest in you as a founder, you have to be able to show enough of yourself for people to be able to connect with you, especially across lines of racial difference, gender difference, and age difference. But that can be so difficult when you feel like those are the things that can expose you or possibly be used against you.

Self-awareness is an invaluable tool for a start-up entrepreneur. Many people are familiar with SWOT analysis, a way of mapping the strengths, weaknesses, opportunities, and threats. Companies often conduct these to analyze the viability of a new strategy or plan. It could be helpful to do a personal SWOT analysis, not for your company, but for yourself. Knowing how systems work is critically important for navigating them effectively. We can't plan for something we don't know exists. Melanie advocates for stepping back, depersonalizing the challenges, and thinking about ourselves as part of a system.

My graduate work was in organizational development; that's where I gained an appreciation for systems-thinking. Until we burn this whole thing down and build something new, we have to work within the system that exists, or at least be mindful as we engage with it. If you come into any system and you push, it will resist you. That's what they're built to do. Not all of it is malicious. People don't like change. What I've seen over and over is when we burst into a new space and start pushing, the pushback feels like we're in quicksand, being labeled problematic, and feeling like you are slowly being deflated, like all the burdens of society are pressing down on your career prospects. Some people just bend and flex to become whatever they need to be to get to the next level. But others, who can't bear the thought of twisting and contorting, have to find another way. They either exit or—an even better path—leverage community and gatekeepers to unlock the doors.

On this point, both Krystal and Bea offered a similar warning, which is to avoid placing the brunt of the responsibility on the oppressed or marginalized individual to transform the systems that have denied them power and access. The effect of trauma cannot be underestimated. Krystal described to me how an experience like being ridiculed in front of classmates for a wrong answer, while just one event in a girl's life, can be so scarring it causes her to shrink in any other settings in the future when a similar fear is present or she perceives the potential to be humiliated. Consider the long-term psychological impacts of being made to feel less worthy because of something you have no power to change, something you cannot control or keep quiet. This fear travels with you into every room, into every interaction.

Not everyone has a particularly traumatic or psychologically damaging childhood. It's true many girls are raised in affirming, equitable households and grow up to choose life partners who believe in the fair distribution of labor at home. No, not every woman internalizes the blatant and subversive presence of misogyny in most societies or operates under the belief that being a woman makes her any less capable or worthy. Of course, there are exceptions. To look for exceptions, though, is to miss the point.

Sometimes, I just want to channel my childhood best friend Julie, an Afro-Latina, and scream, "Basta, ya!" in Spanish, like she did when she got annoyed. "'Enough, already!'" Enough of not stating the obvious. Enough of not making room for the admission of things that only hurt us when we hold them in. There's a better, brighter tomorrow if we let the acceptance that it's harder open the way. This is my attempt to get the conversation started, and I hope you'll keep it going in real life.

Far better to acknowledge that individually and collectively, aspects of the experience of being born a girl and growing into a woman are idiosyncratic and demand consideration. If we can agree this is worth acknowledging, then we might also agree speaking about the things that seem taboo could help hasten our progress in addressing and eliminating the barriers. We explore that in the next chapter.

CHAPTER 7:

TALK ABOUT THE TABOO STUFF

———

Women are half the population, and yet it's still considered taboo to speak about everyday experiences like having our period, the challenges of becoming pregnant and adjusting to motherhood, or the grief of losing a child. Tabloids pay top dollar to get the first look at a celebrity's newborn baby, but a woman who publicly acknowledges and shares her pain over a stillbirth is vilified. Something is wrong when we make such significant parts of our life unmentionable. We can change that by speaking ourselves fully into existence and talking about the taboo stuff.

LET'S TALK ABOUT PERIODS

When I was growing up, *The Cosby Show* was more than entertainment. It was an education. Faithfully on Thursday evenings, I tuned in to watch Phylicia Rashad's character, Clair Huxtable. Mrs. Huxtable graced my screen each week in all her fabulous glory, making fashion statements. Yet she was most memorable and influential for the subtle yet unmistakable cultural and social statements she made. Her mere existence on television as a robust, nuanced portrayal of a Black wife, mother, attorney, former college friend, and woman was statement enough.

There were women like her, and I could grow up to be one. I was obsessed with her perfectly coiffed hair, flawless skin, impeccable diction, and command of multiple languages. Setting aside the controversy surrounding the show in recent years, Clair is, in my estimation, the enduring legacy and gift of that visionary sitcom. Watching it suspended, even if just for thirty minutes each week, any and all limiting beliefs the world would impose on a family who looked like my own, and on girls and women with skin like mine.

In the episode entitled "The Infantry Has Landed (and They've Fallen Off the Roof)," Rudy, the youngest Huxtable girl whose character was played by Keshia Knight Pulliam, gets her period for the first time. Her mother wants to celebrate her journey to womanhood, and Rudy wants no parts of it. To date, I struggle to recall any other mainstream TV show from my childhood that dealt so realistically and respectfully with the topic of girls and their periods. That episode shaped not just my own thoughts around what it meant not to just accept the steps from girlhood to womanhood, but to honor them. It was poignant for my mother, and I know because she reminded me of it when we watched that episode together some years later.

"I kept fidgeting, and my mom noticed, but I acted like I was fine, still fighting the urge to get up. At some point, though, I just went for it. I quickly found out what all the fuss had been about, and just in time, it seemed. Just like that, I had become a woman."

It happened on a Thursday night, and I know because that was the evening my family attended our weekly Bible study. I was twelve. Because I was studious and also because I genuinely enjoyed what I was learning, I tended to be well-prepared and an enthusiastic participant in these discussions. We used to meet in the private home of a family in our congregation, and my mom and dad frowned upon us going too often to use their bathroom, not that I even really wanted to get up. Usually, our sessions were in the basement of said family's home, and there were these narrow and creaky stairs that made it impossible to discreetly get up and down. Everyone would notice and crane their necks, and it would cause a whole disruption. If that wasn't enough incentive to stay put, my dad was usually the conductor for the study and got annoyed if the noisy kid distracting everyone was one of his own. Basically, my brother and I knew to use the bathroom before we arrived or hold it until we got back home.

This particular evening, though, I was not feeling like myself. For one thing, I was tired, inexplicably so. I also felt a weird sensation like I had to pee, only I knew for certain I didn't have to pee. I kept fidgeting, and my mom noticed, but I acted like I was fine, still fighting the urge to get up. At some point, though, I just went for it. And just in time, it seemed, because I quickly found out why everyone makes such a fuss. Just like that, I had become a woman. Later, my mom asked me what we would do to celebrate. "We'll be like Clair and Rudy," she said. Honestly, I don't remember what we decided to do, but it probably involved a nice lunch that weekend. I do recall, all too well, the introduction to cramps, and we've been getting reacquainted like clockwork every month since.

According to the World Bank's online database, women and girls make up 49.6 percent of the population, which makes the experience of navigating from girlhood to womanhood something that is shared by half of the people in the world. Why then are uniquely female biological happenings still treated as taboo? I've wondered about it so much, and my experiences with founders have demonstrated to me over and over not talking about our experiences as females hurts more than it helps. It doesn't allow us to normalize what we go through or celebrate all we're achieving despite our challenges. What does any of this have to do with succeeding as a woman social entrepreneur? Everything.[18]

Honoring our womanhood is critical to tapping into our feminine power and showing up as our most authentic selves. This isn't about being crass. It's about acknowledging our physical and biological makeup is part of our personhood. If we're discussing women who are solving some of the world's

---

18 The World Bank, "Population, Female (% of Total) Data," September 4, 2020.

most intractable problems, then we must be talking about menstrual health, and that means periods, pregnancy, and motherhood. When we miss that, we miss the most critical and obvious levers in creating a more equitable and inclusive society and opening pathways for women to build and scale their ventures.

Helping Women Period is a nonprofit organization founded by Executive Director Lysne Tait, which supports women and girls who are experiencing homelessness and who would not otherwise have access to feminine products. One article they published states, "From the time of her first cycle to menopause, the average American woman will have around 450 periods in her lifetime." The math is actually startling to consider because, "Added up, this equates to around ten years—or about 3,500 days—of the average woman's life that will be spent menstruating. Translated into period products, this works out at around 11,000 tampons that the average woman uses in a lifetime." Contemplate for a moment, the implications of this monthly occurrence, which starts for most girls at the age of twelve, as it did for me.

My point is not to minimize the transition from boyhood to manhood; the awkwardness, the bodily changes, or the emotional transformations boys go through deserve to be recognized. But the fact remains, nothing young men go through equates to the loss of ten years of their life. Women, from their preteens on, show up to learn, compete in a sport, build companies, and generally persist not just without applause, but with the not-so-subtle message they had better not complain.

I'll never forget sitting in the large conference room with nearly all the members of a corporate communications team. At the time, I worked for a global human development organization that spearheaded programs in more than fifty countries. The focus of much of our work was in East and West Africa, Central America, and the Middle East. Our efforts were increasingly aimed at incorporating a racial and gender equity lens across all of our education, economic, and health portfolios. Our team was an exception to most of the others in the executive suite because we were woman-led and comprised of almost all female-identifying colleagues. I don't remember us ever having more than two men on a team of more than twenty people.

On this particular day, we met to discuss upcoming observation days around the world and to pitch ideas for social marketing campaigns that could help bring awareness to causes our interventions and research helped address. Menstrual Hygiene Day was coming up in late May, and this was especially important to some of our programs serving girls in resource-poor nations. It's a simple problem to fix, which has broad implications. When girls don't have access to menstrual hygiene products, they stay home from school or drop out entirely, which exacerbates the education crisis in many lands and ultimately perpetuates cycles of poverty. UNICEF estimates across the African continent alone, one in ten girls miss school each year due to their period. By miss school, they mean habitually, resulting in anywhere from 10 to 20 percent of lost instructional time.[19]

---

19 Phineas Rueckert, "Why Periods Are Keeping Girls Out of School & How You Can Help," *Global Citizen*, June 30, 2018.

Our team knew all of the statistics on this. We had an opportunity to build a campaign that could lead to greater awareness about the challenges for women and girls around the world related to menstruation, not just in a few poor countries. Some of us around the table were enthusiastically pitching ideas that could help humanize and normalize this issue. To their credit, my male colleagues vocalized strong support and were aghast to understand the magnitude of the problem for which there was such a straightforward solution. Only we didn't get very far.

The most senior women around the table pushed back on every idea that could bring this issue closer to home and ultimately determined not to build a campaign at all but to simply post about it on social media in solidarity. Many of us left the meeting confused and frustrated at the outcome. It was clear to me several of my peers had internalized it was not safe to speak about menstruation, especially not as a woman-led team. I can only imagine how often that scenario plays out. Could this be why our parental leave policies have yet to change and why we still don't have universal childcare? What if it wasn't taboo to care about the health of half the world's population? In the end, one campaign is not a matter of life or death. But for too many women, menstrual health is just that.

LET'S TALK ABOUT PREGNANCY

Arion Long is the founder and chief estrogen officer at Femly, a steadily growing tech-for-good company producing healthy alternatives to toxic feminine care. Along the way, she is breaking down negative stereotypes, particularly those which could compromise Black women's health, and increasing lifesaving education, access, and awareness.

She would know about the importance of all that because it's a miracle Arion is alive. All through her teens and early twenties, she dealt with difficult periods, but she had no idea her monthly routine would almost kill her. She was diagnosed with a cervical tumor at age twenty-six, and when she did more research, she discovered the culprit was likely the store-bought products she used every month.[20]

Shockingly, "90 percent of the feminine products in stores contain unhealthy substances linked to heavy bleeding, endometriosis, and infertility, and even contain dioxin and BPA, both known carcinogens," which is information she both shared in an interview with the web publication I95 Business and often mentions in her talks and pitches for Femly.[21]

Beating cancer is the coup of a lifetime, and yet that wasn't Arion's only brush with death related to her menstrual health. In 2018, as her company was taking off, she suffered the stillbirth of her daughter Sage. Reflecting on how she honors her loss and these life-changing experiences through her entrepreneurial pursuits, she said:

We honor Sage in everything I do. After losing Sage, my feminine care company exploded, but I also included a lot of work

20   Tory Burch Foundation, "Arion Long on Changing Feminine Care–The Embrace Ambition Series," *YouTube* video, 13:13, November 2, 2019.
21   Cheryl Balassone, "Femly Founder Arion Long Is Changing Feminine Care. Period," *I95 Business,* December 10, 2018.

in decreasing maternal mortality. I've worked with Congress to help reduce the rates of Black women dying in pregnancy and labor. So I just pushed through for my baby.[22]

For Arion, pushing through hasn't meant ignoring her pain. Her company exists to help normalize prioritizing their menstrual and maternal health, and hopefully living longer, healthier lives as a result.

LET'S TALK ABOUT PARENTHOOD

"Having my own daughter, while trying to build a company, changed me. The modern workplace wasn't designed for most of us, and we will have to redesign it."—Callan Blount Fleming

Maybe you think these are compelling stories but are still not sure what they mean for you. What does it say about us if we are comfortable operating in a world where it is taboo to talk about feminine health, where we remove from discussion the daily experiences of fifty percent of our population? These women are our wives, partners, colleagues, clients, grantees, and investees, and if we're not considering them in the full context of their life, we aren't really seeing them at all. More than that, in a society that doesn't accommodate the challenges arising from menstrual health, men lose out too.

Callan Blount Fleming is the founder and CEO of Spark Collective, and her company is on a mission to make

---

22   Heather Wilson, "Brave Through Grief: An Interview with Arion Long," *YouTube* video, 22:35, May 9, 2020.

the "future of work" work for everyone, especially working parents. She reflected with me about her tenure as a senior executive at a nonprofit education management organization. It was during an exciting period when they were scaling quickly, and as a people-manager, she had yet to learn how to center people over productivity and process.

In one instance, she recalls with chagrin her own participation in alienating one of the team members who reported to her, a male colleague whose wife had given birth too early while they were traveling out of state. Far from their preferred medical team and home, their daughter arrived safely into the world, and this new father had to shuttle back and forth for weeks between New York City and Washington, DC, where she stayed in the neonatal intensive care unit.

I really botched that one, and while I wish I could say I behaved then the way I coach managers to behave now, I know I didn't. Looking back, that experience has informed so much of my work now. Also, having my own daughter, while trying to build a company, changed me. The modern workplace wasn't designed for most of us, and we will have to redesign it.

In a span of three months during the pandemic, nearly eight hundred thousand women left the workforce, and an overwhelming number of them were moms. Even under relatively normal circumstances, we haven't figured out how to mitigate the dual pressures for employed partners at home and work.

"I read somewhere that each year 43 percent of women leave the workforce, and 43 percent of them are mothers, just like mine. Back in 2014 when I was becoming a mom, I didn't know those numbers."

—KATIE SMITH ROBERTS

I was standing in a very loud atrium in the Washington Hilton, on a bright but quite chilly Friday afternoon, when my phone rang. I excused myself from a conversation and walked briskly to the only spot where I could sort of talk without screaming to take a call I had been anticipating for days. On the other end of the phone was Katie Smith Roberts, the woman who would soon become my boss. She was calling to offer me a job, or at least I hoped. I needed to prepare myself either way, but I had a good feeling about it. Katie was pleasant, and she didn't bury the lead.

"Hi, Danielle. I hope this time still works."

I'm sure it was all the background noise that gave her pause. The conference attendees networking, schmoozing, and bustling about were a bit much for me too, but I didn't have anywhere else to go.

"Yes, please excuse the background noise. It's the best spot I could find here in the hotel," I replied. At this point, I was cupping my phone close to my mouth to make sure she could hear me.

"Well, I won't keep you long. I'm excited to call and offer you the job." I remember her ending the call by saying, "and because I want you to be sure of how much we want you, we added $10,000 to your starting salary offer. It would be great to have your answer by Monday so we can let the other candidates know."

It was one of the easiest decisions I have ever had to make. I remember saying a quick prayer and then basically floating through the rest of the day and into the weekend.

Katie and I were two women in transition. I was relocating to a new city to be closer to my boyfriend, who soon after became my fiancé. Holdjiny proposed to me the evening before my first day of work. All of my clothes and furniture still needed to be unloaded from the moving truck. It was a crazy time, starting a new job and planning a wedding, which we set for just six months away. Unbeknownst to me, Katie was growing her family, literally carrying a new baby boy inside her. Within our first few months working together, she went out on maternity leave, and when she came back, everything had shifted, including her relationship with work and herself. We grew together as humans, as colleagues, and as friends, and I got a front-row seat to her journey from an overwhelmed professional working mom to stay-at-home mom, and later to *momtrepreneur.*

My mother worked incredibly hard raising my two broth-ers and myself, but as a stay-at-home mom, she was finan-cially dependent on my dad. On one occasion, as I listened to my mom list off the things we needed, I noticed she didn't include anything for herself. What I felt could probably best be described as pity. I promised myself I would never be like her. In fact, I ran in quite the opposite direction after college, focusing on building a career."

It wasn't that Katie couldn't think of any benefits to her mom having stayed home with her children. She remembers her mother at her hospital bed as a young girl who needed corrective spinal surgery and many other moments where her mom was present. It's just that she thought her path would be different. Looking back, she now realizes there is a collective naivete for many women professionals about the tradeoffs their colleagues who are moms feel forced to make.

Each year, 43 percent of women leave the workforce, and 43 percent of them are mothers, just like mine. Back in 2014, when my own motherhood journey began, I didn't know those numbers.[23]

Katie was referencing a study done in 2013, just two years before she would become a mom of two and join the ranks of women who leave their jobs because the pressure to be all things to everyone at home and in the office became too much. If this was the reality for a woman like Katie, someone who benefits from many of the privileges that come from being a member of the majority culture, economically secure, married, and having access to childcare, what must it feel like to be a woman trying to make ends meet as the sole breadwinner in a family and living at or just above the poverty line?

---

23   Paulette Light, "Why 43% of Women with Children Leave Their Jobs, and How to Get Them Back," *The Atlantic*, April 19, 2013.

Maybe that's why I felt more sadness than surprise when Katie asked me to meet her in one of the office nooks with the plushy chairs for our check-in one Monday. In retrospect, she probably hoped to soften the blow of hard news by picking the most comfortable and discreet spot on our floor. I couldn't possibly have known how difficult a decision it had been for her to make, but her reflections about the time certainly provide some insight.

When I became pregnant with my first son, I expected there would be challenges, but I was entirely unprepared for how tough it would be. I clung to the idea I could continue to work in the same way and at the same pace I had for over a decade. I wasn't ready to concede, so I just kept going. I ignored what my body was trying to tell me. I put myself last. That worked for a time. Then, something broke in me quite literally when my second son was born—physically, emotionally, and mentally.

As she made the tough decision to join the 43 percent of women who leave the workforce, she remembers thinking about her mom. She wondered how it could be possible that society had not budged in its expectations for women in an entire generation.

It turns out I wasn't superhuman. I wasn't the first, nor would I be the last, professional mom to nearly kill herself before admitting that truth either. To acknowledge this reality meant maybe I had been wrong in how I viewed my mom's choices. Through it all, I kept wondering: was this how my mom had felt? How could this still be the only choice for moms all these years later?

Katie and I stayed connected over the next year because we were founding members of Tide Risers, an intentional community of women who are bound together through a yearlong cohort experience aimed to help them amplify their impact through peer coaching and personal development. During that year, I found the courage to also leave my full-time job as managing director of communications and launch She Thinks Purple. Katie was one of my first clients. Unable to accept the few and unfortunate options available to working moms, she was ready to do something about it.

She would design the first coworking space made for moms by a mom and disrupt the still-booming and male-dominated industry. Before we witnessed the rise and decline of titans like WeWork or the launch of women-centric workspaces like The Wing and Luminary, Katie was already dreaming up The Delta. Her workspace would be modeled not for cookie-cutter scalability but for the nourishment, care, and edification of its members: the women who care for their families and often put themselves last.

In reality, it's good business to give moms what we deserve. We women represent formidable buying power. In the average American household, mothers control 85 percent of the purchasing decisions, spending $2.4 trillion annually. Still, companies too often overlook moms.[24] *Even an industry that grew in response to the desire for more flexibility in work has an embarrassing track record with working mothers. To date, the only coworking space I know of that is intentionally designed*

---

24 Jill Krasny, "Infographic: Women Control the Money in America," *Business Insider*, February 17, 2012.

by a mom for moms is my own, The Delta. I believe that is why moms will always come here first when given other choices.

The Delta opened its doors in the midst of a pandemic and has emerged as a solution for working parents who are navigating the need for safe, social-distanced productivity. It's not lost on Katie. Her business model doesn't solve problems for all moms, and there remain many barriers to women of marginalized identities. The Delta is one piece of the solution, and it only exists because Katie decided it was time to bring the conversation so many women have privately into the open, to acknowledge, as she often says, "Moms are heroes, but we're not superhuman."

As the world has changed, rapidly and irrevocably, in complexity, I've found comfort in knowing my values keep me steady. I started this journey for moms like me, and I know now it's simply not enough. What about the moms who aren't at all like me, who have fewer resources and less positional power in society to demand what they deserve? How do I build a company that does not simply recreate the same societal disparities and inequalities which have led us to where we are? I don't have all the answers, but I'm asking much better questions.

Last I checked, women are still getting periods, getting pregnant, and becoming moms. We didn't even discuss menopause, ageism, and how biases sideline women in midlife. Even when everything goes as planned, there are challenges. Too often, though, that's not the case. Black women still have unacceptably high rates of death during childbirth, and younger and younger women are being diagnosed with breast and ovarian cancer. Those who deliver healthy babies face challenges with inflexible work environments, and we all suffer from societal norms that police what we're allowed to discuss.

What seems clear to me is unless we start talking about much of what's considered taboo, we will miss opportunities to innovate and create the future we all deserve. We are the total of all of our experiences, and we cannot subscribe to the belief that some parts of our personhood are banned. Let's not lose any more time being silent. Talk about the taboo stuff.

CHAPTER 8:

MAKE A PLAN FOR SURVIVING THE TERRIBLE TWOS

———

Businesses, like babies, go through developmental stages. While no two are the same, there are themes and patterns. When my company turned two, it felt like I was going through what some parents describe as the *terrible twos*, when their sweet babies turn into not-so-sweet toddlers. It's a phase where everything that used to work is suddenly obsolete, and you need all-new skills to manage. What I needed more than anything else was a set of new tools for managing my emotions, my time, and my expectations of myself and others.

Once we know what to expect, it can be much easier to navigate through the challenges. Looking back, I can identify three missteps that made an already difficult period even more overwhelming. Not surprisingly, when I asked other women, they experienced similar setbacks. Hopefully, our collective insights can help you feel more ready, so that you can chart your own path. Let our words help you make a plan that doesn't just get you through but also sets you up for future success.

FIRST, I APPROACHED MY DAILY LIFE LIKE I WAS STILL WORKING A FULL-TIME JOB, NOT RUNNING A COMPANY FULL-TIME.

In my previous gigs (jobs where other people paid me a salary and provided benefits), I specialized in what I was really good at and left all the other jobs to other people who were experts in them. I didn't have to juggle invoicing, bookkeeping, taxes, travel, and reimbursements, along with strategy, business development, and marketing. Now, I had to do all of those jobs. Only I wasn't acting like I had all these jobs. I was still focusing most of my time on the aspects I most enjoyed and felt confident doing, neglecting the other stuff. I also wasn't asking for help or identifying the right people and technology to assist me in creating the right systems and automation. This was bound to catch up with me, and it did. This may seem obvious to some of you, but for many women, it is a real struggle to make the switch from thinking like a worker bee to a boss.

What I hadn't accounted for was all of the hidden work. On this topic, Melissa Rebecca Brogdon, founder of Campbell Impact, said:

There has to be a willingness to work for free when you're working for yourself. I initially thought of my work as the hours I was billing to others for the services I provided, but there's so much hidden work I was doing for myself that was just about building my company and was essentially me working for free. If you're not willing to do that work, then you won't actually have a viable business in the long run.

So much of the labor in leading a start-up social enterprise is invisible and unpaid. It is all this foundational work that creates a platform. You will lose track of how many hours you invest, and you will work abnormal hours. You will think about your work constantly. You will find it strange to disconnect mentally, even when you are unplugged physically. Knowing what to expect can help you plan accordingly. This brings me to the next thing I got all wrong.

SECOND, I MINIMIZED THE UNRELENTING AND ALL-CONSUMING NATURE OF A START-UP AND HOW IT WOULD ZAP MY TIME AND ENERGY.

Returning to the idea of our business as our baby, there's an expectation there will be some sleepless nights and some sacrifice, though there can also be a tendency to glamorize the experience. Because I had done the hard parts of a job before, I expected this would be like all the other times, so I didn't build the habits and practices I would need when things became much more difficult than I could have imagined. I believed I could run a business and be the same wife, daughter, and friend as always. I believed I would have more time and freedom to invest in my fitness, mental health, and overall well-being. Maybe naively, I believed because I was doing mission-driven work, it wouldn't feel like work at all. On every level, I was proven wrong again and again. With each success, like getting a new client or gaining more visibility, there was more work waiting. By year two, it all felt unsustainable and draining. This is totally normal. I just didn't know.

As Darrah Brustein noted in her article "The 20 Hardest Things About Starting a Business," most people who start any enterprise go through much the same things, only most don't share all of the ugly details.

We see a lot of images of cool entrepreneurs who made it big. Most of these business celebrities went through hard times but didn't get the opportunity to talk about them in the media, can't remember them well, or don't want us to know about the hurdles they jumped. This is like the entrepreneurship version of airbrushing: It looks great on paper, but deep down, you know it's fabricated." In the end, she concluded, *"No matter how you frame it, it takes years of hard work to become an "overnight success."*[25]

FINALLY, I DIDN'T HAVE A REAL PLAN.

No, I don't mean a business plan. I didn't have a survival plan. It wasn't that I didn't know there would come a time when the *honeymoon* phase would wear off. I started my company as a newlywed. But simply knowing something is likely to happen is not the same as planning ahead for it. I didn't have a plan for what I would do when things got tough or how I would keep it all in balance. I wasn't creating durable systems to anchor me. A combination of poor operational planning and overextension led to intense burnout, right when my business needed me to grow, adapt, and persist.

---

25   Darrah Brustein, "The 20 Hardest Things About Starting a Business," *Business Collective*, 2016.

She Thinks Purple turned two the same month I pulled off PurpleCON, the conference which had evolved from a two-hour event the year before to a two-day event the following year. I was wholly unprepared for what hit me, and I started to crash. That experience was one of the reasons I decided to write this book. I wondered, like many parents of little ones in their terrible twos stage: Why did I ever think this was a good idea? Was I really cut out for this? How did anyone survive this?

But I didn't try to tough it out alone. I did what I tend to do when I need help. I turned to Google. I researched and reached out to other founders, especially women entrepreneurs who had been successful or who were further along in their journey. I also engaged an executive coach, DeDee Cai, whose holistic coaching practice, Fit To Profit, helped me regain some perspective and gave me new tools. Our sessions helped me identify what was holding me back and how I could train my mind and habits the way one trains physically.

DeDee has seen firsthand how taking a lackadaisical approach to planning ahead for when things get hard leads so many founders to burnout, from which they may never recover. She knows because she's been there, feigning happiness because things looked much better from the outside than she felt on the inside. When her clients come to her, she says they often fit the following description.

They feel like they're bad at business. They are searching for all the blogs and all the content they can get their hands on from so-called experts because they think they are missing something. They've been working hard and doing everything other people tell them about how to succeed as an entrepreneur. They've hit a wall and aren't sure they can keep up the pace or facade any longer. They don't have the stamina to keep going. They feel burnt out. The worst part is that they started their company to build something meaningful in the world. They dream about a better life. They're literally about to give up, throw in the towel, but then decide to give it one more try. That's where I come in.

Have you been there? Are you feeling and thinking some of those things right now? If nobody else has told you, I will now: you are normal. You are allowed to feel all of those things. This moment will pass, and there will probably be future moments like it. Here are some perspectives on how to weather the storm. All these words are from founders who, just like you, are flawed. They are no strangers to failure, and yet they are fiercely committed to their vision.

FACE YOUR NEW REALITY

If you've made it this far, I commend you. Now recommit to your business, remember why you started the company in the first place, and refill your tank. Whatever got you to this point has likely already been used up (money, network, drive). You need new tools, new reasons to believe, and new relationships to help you break through.

Especially if you're leading tech for a good start-up (but even if you're not), I suggest you read *Mechanical Bull: How You Can Achieve Startup Success* by Cheryl Contee. After sharing sage advice on how to navigate the wild ride of launching a start-up, as a woman and person of color under the scrutiny of a mostly male gaze, she closes with a sobering remark from a friend: "more people have been to the moon than black women who have successfully executed their tech start-ups."[26] The reality is most start-ups don't make it this far, and yet you're here. Embrace that you are here and let it fuel you to keep going.

RESIST THE URGE TO COMPARE YOURSELF TO OTHERS

Nod your head if any of these statements apply to you:

- Your bank account is getting thinner as your friends are celebrating their bonuses earned at fancy corporate jobs.
- Everybody you know (at least according to Instagram) is taking fabulous vacations and posting pictures of mouth-watering meals they're eating oceanside in exotic places, except you.
- You're starting to think maybe this wasn't the right decision, and it's not worth it, especially since your family and friends still don't quite get what you're building or don't understand how long it takes, and you feel like you have to defend yourself to them.

Fight the urge to edit your vision or to compare yourself to anyone else. Doing so is a waste of your precious energy. Many businesses fail within one, two, or five years, but that doesn't have to be you. Among the ones that make it, there's a common denominator: a founder who never gave up or gave in to the idea they wouldn't succeed.

---

26 Cheryl Contee, *Mechanical Bull: How You Can Achieve Startup Success* (New York: Lioncrest Publishing, 2019).

When you decide to give into #FOMO, watch the TEDx Talk "The Culture of Comparison" by Bea Arthur, founder of The Difference, a tech company delivering on-demand mental health solutions. As a serial entrepreneur who found success in her more than decade-long quest to change the world through business, she knows that comparing ourselves to others is a losing game. She says many quotable things in her talk, but these words have always helped me:

That's what the culture of comparison does; it causes you to grade your own choices against other people. But I can tell you nothing else in this world will make you more confused or paralyzed than basing your choices and opinions on those of others.

Darrah Brustein started her first company when she was laid off, even though she was outperforming her colleagues. She decided if doing all the right things could still leave her jobless, it was time to take back control. With expertise across industries, including media, financial literacy, education technology, professional networking, and career development, she leads two accelerator programs for women in businesses. When I asked her about the key to persevering in entrepreneurship despite the challenges, she said this:

I wish someone had told me, in the end, my success would have much more to do with being persistent, consistent, and resilient than anything else. A lot of days, you simply won't feel like doing what needs to be done, even small things, and you will be frustrated, maybe even crying. Pushing through on those days and showing up consistently over time is how you build resilience. You will figure the other stuff out.

ELIMINATE CLUTTER FROM YOUR LIFE

Don't hold onto anything that's not serving you at this moment. Parents of toddlers give away old baby clothes, toys, and supplies to make room for all the new stuff their kid needs. Old stuff just gets in their way. It's unnecessary clutter. Your clutter can be anything: bad habits (not eating right, sleeping enough, or getting enough exercise), unreasonable expectations you're still holding onto (trying to be the perfect anything), or just clunky and inefficient business processes that worked when you were much smaller but could never work now. It could be people who started out with you but aren't the right people or in the right roles. You might need to get out of your own way. If you need some inspiration on how and what to let go, read *Drop the Ball: Achieving More by Doing Less* by Tiffany Dufu.

Tiffany was gracious enough to give me a few minutes of her time as I was writing this book. She has entered a select club of women (and even smaller for Black women) who have raised over a million dollars for their start-ups, and in her case, approaching five million dollars. As the founder and CEO of The Cru, she's scaling her vision for a tech-enabled community that helps accelerate women personally and professionally through the power of group coaching relationships. Of the things she had to drop to succeed, she comments the most important thing was letting go of attempting to manage what other people thought of her as a way to modulate the level of racism or sexism she may encounter.

It's ultimately about efficiency. When you commit to showing up as your authentic self in every situation, with everyone, then you no longer have to keep track of all these separate versions of yourself. It's exhausting to have to remember which pieces of you to take off at the door and to collect and put back on at the end of each day. When you're always you, you get back so much time and energy that could go to better use.

Now is as good a time as any to do some inventory. Is there any physical or metaphorical junk in your life? Do you need to do some decluttering? Do your best Marie Kondo impression and toss out anything not bringing you joy or bringing you closer to your dreams.

REDISCOVER YOUR UNIQUE STRENGTHS

If your business is a toddler, that means you haven't killed her. You're doing at least something right. Now would be a good time to examine your unique strengths and find support in the areas where you are weak. Are you exceptional at winning new business, marketing, or product development but lacking other critical skills? Maybe consider bringing on a cofounder or looking for ways to automate aspects of your operations that drain your time and energy. Just remember, everyone has a superpower, and no one has a monopoly on what it takes to succeed in business.

You don't have to go it alone. Join a community where you can network with other entrepreneurs. Read biographies of people who have overcome similar odds, being mindful not to compare yourself but, instead, seek to take away only what serves you. Don't get caught up in the *hustle hype*. Whenever you're feeling like an outsider or the underdog, remember these words from Brandice Daniel's TEDxMemphis Talk "The Real Winners Are on the Outside": "If you had the idea, the idea is for you." So that means stop doubting yourself. She continues, "Being an outsider is a gift . . . the world needs your idea."[27]

Never forget you made the decision to launch this endeavor because you saw a solution to a problem, and you had a vision. You have the unique advantage of being the only human who sees the world precisely as you do. Now would be a great time to get reacquainted with the three things you were clear on from the beginning: who you are, what your values are, and where you're going. If you haven't heard this in a while: you are enough.

WORK ON YOUR MINDSET EVERY DAY

Your brain can be your best friend or your worst enemy. Deep down, she only wants what's best for us. But the downside to her being so overprotective is she can sometimes talk us out of things that are really good for us because they seem dangerous. That's why we must all work on mindset, training our thoughts to work for us and not against us. Whenever you feel you're losing hope, that you are spiraling downward, seek comfort and inspiration in others' stories. Go back and read some of the stories from this book. Remember, you're not the first person to feel what you feel or to question what you're questioning.

For me, listening to Sara Blakely tell the story of how she went from a fax machine saleswoman to founder and CEO

27 Brandice Daniel, "The Real Winners Are on the Outside," filmed at TEDxMemphis, video, 8:45.

of Spanx on NPR's *How I Built This* podcast was a turning point. With the motivation to wear a ninety-eight-dollar pair of cream-colored paints that had been sitting in her closet for months, the determination to create a better life for herself, $5,000 in personal savings, and one person who was willing to help her with her *crazy idea*, Sara launched the company that made her the youngest billionaire in America.[28]

The breakthrough I experienced listening to Sara's process of building her underwear empire was I needed to be more intentional about my mindset. Across her social media, she often discusses why learning how was life-changing.

Mindset is to an entrepreneur what physical strength and capacity are to an athlete. It's the single most important skill you can have. Being an entrepreneur is about handling obstacles, day-in and day-out. Your mindset is your greatest asset. Work on it all the time. Get your hands-on motivational stuff wherever you can because how you react to anything will ultimately change the course for everything.

Make a plan, your survival plan, for how you will get through the difficult times. The best time to plan for challenges is before they happen. Naturally, there are some things we simply cannot ever predict. Who knew an invisible airborne virus would claim over a million and bring the global economy to a halt for months? This is the thing of Hollywood imagination and movie plots, and yet it became all of our reality almost overnight.

---

28   Sara Blakely, "Spanx: How I Built This with Guy Raz," NPR, July 3, 2017.

No, making a plan won't isolate us from the storms. With the right business practices, habits, and mindsets, though, we can stay anchored and steady through them. Beyond planning for the worst, successful entrepreneurs are always on the lookout for unexpected opportunities. So let's explore how you can invite more serendipity into your life.

CHAPTER 9:

CREATE YOUR OWN SERENDIPITY

———

*"Risk-taking, trust, and
serendipity are key ingredients of
joy. Without risk, nothing new
ever happens. Without trust, fear
creeps in. Without serendipity,
there are no surprises."*

—RITA GOLDEN GELMAN

Sometimes I get curious about a word and go down the rabbit hole that is the internet in search of answers. Apparently, we have Horace Walpole to thank for the addition of the word serendipity to the English language. He first used the word in a letter in 1754, noting he derived the term from a "silly fairy tale" about three Persian princes who sailed off to an island called Serendip in pursuit of riches. Today we know Serendip as the island of Sri Lanka, and many use the word serendipity to refer to delightful encounters that come about through happenstance.[29]

With time, some have come to conflate serendipity with luck, which I think is a mistake. Luck must rely on some mystical power from a source over which we have no control. The power to create the conditions for serendipity is within our own hands. Entrepreneurs, especially, should master the art of creating serendipity. Each day we have the opportunity for enriching and delightfully unplanned encounters. These interactions often spark our creativity and challenge our thinking in ways that open new possibilities for our social ventures. Here are three proven ways to create your own serendipity, based upon my experiences and those of other women like you.

SMILE AT STRANGERS

I say this with a few caveats, recognizing we live in a scary world where not everyone wishes us well. Still, we must do unexpected things to have unexpected results. Maybe we've gotten into the habit of looking unapproachable because we want to block any unwelcome attention, mostly from strange men on the street. I'm with you. Catcalling and inappropriate advances are not cool. It's possible, though, by looking unapproachable, we're also shutting down conversation from polite strangers who could be potential clients or helpful connections. You know better than me what will work for you, and I invite you to be reasonable and use discretion. Also,

---

29   Jess Zafarris, "The Etymology of 'Serendipity,'" *Useless Etymology*, December 2, 2017.

consider if you could send out friendlier vibes by smiling and greeting others as you move through the day in safe spaces.

Before the pandemic outbreak, I often traveled via Amtrak from Washington, DC to New York City. On an early morning trip, while waiting for the cafe car to open, a stranger sat across from me—a tall, slim, middle-aged white guy. Typically, I don't enjoy conversations with anyone before 8:30 a.m., let alone someone I don't know. We both smiled and greeted each other. That turned into a conversation. He had owned a successful management consulting company for nearly twenty years. He was incredibly generous and interested in my work.

During this impromptu session, he gave me tips on shifting toward a value-based pricing model for my services. At one point, he even helped me wordsmith a new template email to work from whenever I was setting up pricing conversations in the future. I still use some of the strategies he shared with me. In about thirty minutes, I tapped into years of expertise. Smiling and saying hello cost me nothing. What I got in exchange was priceless. I'll never know what prompted his interest in me or the random act of kindness that followed, and our paths may not cross again in an intentional way. Still, I'm grateful for our serendipitous meeting. It's not just me, though. Here's another example:

Who in your life can you recognize by the sound of their laugh? Can you think of someone whose laughter makes jokes even funnier? I know a few people like that, and one of them is Lois Sarfo-Mensah. It's no surprise she cites joy as both an intention and a value that guides her event strategy and logistics management company, 3 Pillars Co. She's an exuberant woman, and she's someone who comes immediately to mind when I think about the power of a smile to spark the most serendipitous events.

Lois and I were strangers just two years ago, and she's become a trusted advisor and partner. We have Crystal Mosby, founder of Tinted and a mutual friend, to thank for making the introduction. Whether she is curating networking events as the co-chair for Ladies Get Paid Baltimore, making new business connections for emerging restaurateurs, or facilitating internships for students from her alma mater University of Maryland Baltimore County (UMBC), I have witnessed firsthand how Lois' sincere interest in other people has attracted clients, contracts, and business connections. Often, these engagements start with nothing more than her bright, contagious smile and a sincere hello.

I'm naturally a people-person, but some of this is subconscious. People seem to show up at my door unexpectedly, and I'm not always sure how or why they find me. Other people see my friendliness and my openness more than I see it in myself. I don't plan to smile at people or start random conversations, but almost all of my business has come from networking. Some of my clients have told me they chose me over another vendor because they liked I was relaxed, transparent, and they felt like they would enjoy their experience.

Lois has set an intention that goes against what many people experience in her industry. By her own admission, one might not readily associate events, logistics, and operations with social impact, but for her, it's about making work less harmful to people. She started her company out of necessity after being laid off by a former employer from a job where she felt overburdened and undervalued, despite being a top performer.

Her company, 3 Pillars Co., is a flat organization where Lois prefers to broker partnerships with newer companies and help them scale by subcontracting them out on larger projects. She focuses on ways to invest back into Black and women-led businesses, and she also recruits college students from the greater Baltimore area from all backgrounds to staff her events. If you scanned the room ahead of an event Lois was producing, as I did when I engaged her to manage a nonprofit gala, you might only sense she was in charge by the people in constant motion around her, checking in and getting approvals. You would notice the incredible diversity across age, gender, and background of her team. All of this is a testament to her openness.

With Lois, anyone can have an opportunity; whether you're a retired grandma or a burly young college football player, Lois insists on deputizing everyone on her team to lead, to innovate, and to decide. She believes the most unexpected things happen when people are happy at work, and she thinks organizations with less hierarchy are the happiest of them all.

Every employer I had in the (events) industry set unrealistic-bordering-on-inhumane expectations and goals, and they always did so under the mask of good intention. That led to burnout and me losing my joy and my passion for the work I otherwise loved. That's why I set joy as my intention in everything I do at 3 Pillars Co. Passion creates joy for me. I try to work on things I'm passionate about and bring people onto my team who are passionate about what we do, and it makes the process more joyful, and our end product is so much better.

Smile, folks, not because I'm telling you to but because you want to attract the best people and energy to move you toward your goals. When you let the joy inside you radiate outward, you won't be able to stop the serendipity from flowing.

GO OUTSIDE

There's a Ghanaian proverb that loosely states, "You must get out of your house to learn." I continuously find new ways in which this proverb is instructive. Our house may be the physical space in which we're working each day. It may also be a figurative space we occupy mentally and emotionally. We must get out of our house daily to keep learning, growing, and advancing. Our house may also be our worldview, informed by our cultural and social networks. We must get out of this house, going beyond what's comfortable and easy to forge new connections and uproot closely held but ultimately unhealthy biases.

We must get into the habit of periodically going outside our daily routines, putting ourselves in spaces that provoke, inspire, and educate. Schedule visits to a local museum, theater performance, or cultural activity where you know you're likely to encounter folks of a different background. Start learning a new language. Take a fifteen-minute walk each day around your own neighborhood, being mindful of greeting at least one neighbor. Join a diverse community where you'll have close proximity to people from various professional backgrounds. When I found my professional network, though full of amazing women, was becoming homogenous, I sought out diverse communities of women leaders, which I found valuable in helping me get out of my proverbial house.

How does a woman go from being a nonprofit communications manager to a founder and an executive producer of an award-winning animation studio whose work has amassed more than four billion views across platforms, whose original film has premiered at Sundance, and who has been named one of *Fast Company*'s 100 Most Creative People in Business in just five years? She certainly doesn't get there by keeping her talent to herself, avoiding risks at all costs, and staying inside.

When Jess Peterson was getting Mighty Oak off the ground, she was the definition of an industry outsider, and she had no idea what the *right* way to market herself was, so she did what she knew. She put herself out there the old school way, just like she had as a kid on the playground selling mixtapes. This time, though, she printed business cards and started attending relevant networking events in New York City. Jess would walk right up to people she'd never met, start a conversation, and leave them with her card. This is not to minimize the courage and confidence it took to do this, but she would be the first to confess it wasn't exactly an ironclad business development strategy. Her willingness to be uncomfortable, to go outside of her comfort zone to build new relationships, along with her incredible talent, has paid off.

Within their first three years, Jess and her partners, Emily Collins and Michaela Olsen, were already pulling in over one million dollars in revenue, and they haven't looked back. Their client roster is full of media heavyweights like Netflix, HBO, NBC, Airbnb, Etsy, Condé Nast, Adult Swim, and *The New York Times*. Jess is a great example of the necessity of going beyond whatever limits us in achieving our dreams. Mighty Oak has used their handcrafted animation techniques to give personality to products and ideas, engaging audiences in unexpected ways.

When we started this company, we had more questions than answers. But thanks to the community we have cultivated over the last few years, we've found ways to achieve goals we didn't know we had and share that success with others. No matter who you are or how you identify, your network is imperative to building your company because they help build you up as well.

Go outside, ladies. That's where the opportunity is, that's where your people are, and they are waiting for you.

MENTOR SOMEONE

Most of us have heard it said that "time is money." That's what makes giving our time such an incredible act of generosity. Like money, when invested well, time can lead to a bigger return in the future. Thankfully, it doesn't take much time or commitment to mentor others. For some, a fifteen-minute conversation, email exchange, or quick text checking on them or sharing a helpful resource goes a long way. Generosity begets generosity. A sure way to have more unexpected, delightful encounters in your life is to generously give your time and knowledge to others. You'll be amazed by how quickly good things come back to you.

There are also many opportunities to forge a connection, whether in-person or through virtual events. By making room in my schedule to offer my expertise to others, the most serendipitous things have happened as a result. The women I've met through communities like Ellevate Network, Tide Risers, and The Cru have become coaches, mentors, friends, clients, and partners. New people who enter our lives bring with them new ways of seeing things.

Reading an email from Erin Perkins changed how I thought about my role in curating experiences that were diverse and inclusive. Before I met Erin, I was operating with a major blind spot. I didn't recognize all the ways events and programs I designed were inaccessible to people with disabilities. Erin reached out to express interest in being part of the inaugural cohort of Tide Risers DC, which I would be leading if we could arrange for an ASL interpreter for the group. Her email caught me off-guard, but it felt like the only equitable answer was yes. This is not a self-congratulatory reflection on my response. The real story is the generosity, openness, and sensitivity Erin embodied as she joined our community and the selflessness and patience she showed in mentoring me and others.

Among the cohort, 60 percent of the women were full-time entrepreneurs, and the other 40 percent worked for an employer and either had a side-hustle they hoped would one day become their main gig or were incubating a new idea they hoped to monetize. As a group of mostly able-bodied women, though some of us were living with less perceptible disabilities, we were all leaving money on the table by not having a strategy for making our business accessible. Erin started to see her unique perspective could be incredibly lucrative, and over our year-long program, she began to experiment with new services geared at teaching founders how to make their companies more accessible. The same woman who had emailed me months prior and requested a scholarship because her own agency hadn't quite taken off yet was now moving decidedly in a more profitable direction. Several members of the community have become her clients.

Some of you may hesitate to offer yourself as a mentor, especially if it requires educating people about some aspect of your identity. Too often, the expectation is that women and people of color are expected to perform unpaid labor as de facto diversity, equity, and inclusion (DEI) counselors. To be constantly reminded of the ways you are different from a group can be exhausting. Having your actual technical expertise ignored and facing interrogation about topics you feel far less qualified to speak on simply because of the way you look can be frustrating.

I know the irritation of being the only Black woman in a room and having other non-black women pepper me with all the burning questions they could have easily Googled on their own. Yep, sometimes random people touch and examine my hair without my permission like I'm an animal at the petting zoo. Of course, I've found myself on the spot with questions about where and I how grew up, and not in a genuinely curious way to establish commonality but in a condescending way that seeks to confirm stereotypes. On other occasions, I've had to defend or speak for all Black people on any number of topics when it's impossible for me to represent any other human's perspective on my own.

Knowing what it has felt like to be othered, I did not feel entitled to know Erin's intimate stories and experiences as a woman who was deaf. It was not her job to educate the rest of us on accessibility. It was a gift to me and so many other women in our community that she offered herself as a mentor, and in the end, it created a most welcome, though unanticipated, opportunity for her. Because this happened on her terms, it was even more powerful. Erin was in control of how she positioned herself and her expertise, and because the value she offered was undeniable, she generated a new market for her services.

When I was in my first breakout group with all Black women, I initially felt self-conscious because I was the only white woman. Within that hour, I realized how much more I had in common with those women than I could ever have imagined, and I knew I was in the right place. As I listened to them talk about sometimes existing in two different worlds, I thought about my experience moving between the deaf community and the hearing community. Because I can speak, I have certain advantages the average deaf person doesn't have, and I feel caught between two worlds sometimes, like when I host dinners and I see the awkwardness between my deaf and hearing friends.

Up to that point, it had not occurred to Erin she had a unique perspective to offer in her business. Her former bosses made her feel as though her disability was a disadvantage she needed to overcome to be a strong contributor. Over time, she became less confident. Now she was looking at herself differently and starting to see how much she had to offer others. It was empowering.

The women in my group were a mirror for me. I can blend in and people might not know I'm deaf. None of the Black women in the group could do that. But why did I feel like I wanted to blend in anyway? Being deaf is just a part of me, a part of my story. That was the start for me in really exploring what was special about my experience. What did I have to teach? Everything changed from that day on, and the more I explored my identity, the more I shared, and the more I helped others, the clearer my own vision became about the company I wanted to lead. I knew it would look totally different than anything I was doing before. That experience changed my life.

Mentor someone. Look for ways you can support your peers, those coming behind you and even those farther ahead, by sharing your perspective and insights. It's great to plug into communities where you can engage in this sharing, but it doesn't always have to be so formal. As with anything, trust your gut, be intentional, and take good care of yourself.

Let's say it again for the people in the back. There's so much we can't control in life, so let's embrace the things we can control. We can smile, greet people, and start conversations with strangers like Lois. We can go outside, opening ourselves up to the world of inspiration and opportunity like Jess. We can mentor someone else, sharing what we've learned through our personal or professional experiences like Erin. Whichever of these options we choose, serendipity awaits.

CHAPTER 10:

LEAD LIKE A WOMAN

—

"That was the day I learned that my first instinct was the right one. I learned to trust my inner voice. I learned to stand up for myself. But somehow, in the intervening twenty-odd years, I had lost touch with that fierce little girl. I'd grown accustomed to listening to and prioritizing the voices of others instead of prioritizing my own."

—TIFFANY DUFU

The future of leadership is female. While it is true we see more visible examples of male leadership in media, business, and society than we do women, representation in leadership is changing, and so are attitudes. Nearly 90 percent of millennials across genders prefer leadership traits typically associated with women. In his 2012 TEDx Talk, John Gerzema, co-author of *The Athena Doctrine: How Women (and the*

Men Who Think Like Them) Will Rule the Future, provides a look into the current shifting views on leadership and society, which his book explores.[30]

Gerzema and fellow author Michael D'Antonio conducted interviews and surveys with more than 64,000 people across thirteen geographically, economically, and culturally diverse countries. In addition, they conducted a global listening tour with stops in twenty-six cities from New York, USA to Nairobi, Kenya, and Tel-Aviv, Israel to Tokyo, Japan. Both men are proud dads interested in how the world will be a more inclusive and progressive place for their own daughters, but more than that, they are social scientists seeking to understand how changes in societal beliefs will shape business trends. They asked people about their beliefs about the world and their confidence in the future regarding leadership and discovered that, across humanity, there is a widespread dissatisfaction with masculine leadership and a collective calling for new rules and a new paradigm.

There's a growing shift in the values between masculinity and femininity in the twenty-first century. We live in a world that's increasingly socially interdependent and transparent, and in this world, feminine values are ascendant because we see the most innovative people among us are breaking from traditional structures to be more flexible, more nurturing, and more collaborative. This is what we call the Athena Doctrine, named after the Greek warrior whose wisdom and civility guided the Greek mythology in this context. We now see people using their femininity in ways large and small to make the world a better place.

---

30   John Gerzema, "The Athena Doctrine," YouTube video, 15:18, October 1, 2012.

If there was ever a time to lead like a woman, that time is now. According to Gerzema and D'Antonio, two out of three people globally think the world would be a better place if men thought more like women. Over the course of a series of surveys and conversations with people across the globe, they found men and women associated being decisive, analytical, proud, and independent with masculine leadership, and associated descriptors like reasonable, collaborative, selfless, expressive, intuitive, and loyal with feminine leadership. When respondents ranked the characteristics they preferred, a vast majority selected the qualities seen as feminine.

It can be challenging to own, hone, and grow our feminine leadership when the most dominant examples of successful entrepreneurs are men. How, then, do we close the authenticity gap in our leadership? I asked a few women who have been successful in owning, honing, and growing their feminine leadership powers, and while their perspectives do not nearly encompass the full breadth of this topic, I believe they offer clear and helpful insights. A few themes emerged from my conversations with several women at various stages in their entrepreneurial careers and across three generations. You will likely notice each one took her own distinct path to embrace feminine qualities. Together, their reflections help us envision how a new paradigm for leadership could look.

START WITH YOUR PRESENCE

When we believe ourselves and speak with conviction, something quite wonderful happens; other people believe us too. As we've already established, confidence doesn't come naturally or equally to everyone. We know we can become more confident with practice. My goal in this chapter is to help you unpack the stuff of leadership and to consider how embracing more innately feminine characteristics of leadership can lead to increased confidence.

Tiffany Dufu often says her purpose on this earth is to advance women and girls, and when you look at her resume, it's clear she has been living that purpose with consistency throughout her professional life. Across her illustrious career in higher education, philanthropy, and now as the founder and CEO of a growing technology start-up, she has always been on a mission to ensure women and girls are seen, supported, and set up for success.

She is someone with whom I can only speak in superlatives, and every interaction with her only deepens my admiration. If female leadership were a magazine, she would be the cover model, and that's why I reached out to her to understand better how she has come to be who she is and what lessons she has learned along the way. Per usual, she had a bright smile, flawless makeup, and phenomenally warm energy for our early morning Zoom interview. She started by honestly admitting she is still in progress.

Leading from an authentic place is something I now do naturally, but I have grown into my leadership over my life and career. This didn't just happen by accident. Throughout my life, people have been teaching me how to show up whether I knew they were teaching me or not. I think this is a very important point. In different stages, my leadership manifested differently, and I was certainly not always the leader I am today.

Tiffany's first model of female leadership was her own mother. She credits her mom with providing what she calls "the first critical intervention" in her life to make it possible for her to become the woman and leader she is today. As a nineteen-year-old expectant mother, Tiffany's mom was able to intuit the only way to change the life outcomes for her child would be to leave Watts, Los Angeles.

It was a rough time in the 1970s, but she felt like there was something other than what she saw around her and used the resources available to her, like her uncle, who was an army recruiter. Together, they convinced my dad to join the army, and I was born nine months later at Fort Lewis army base in Tacoma, Washington. Because of my mother's leadership, my parents broke a vicious cycle of poverty, addiction, and violence in one generation.

That's not nearly all Tiffany's mom did to help her develop what would become her leadership prowess. She describes the way her mom helped both her daughters develop their sense of self:

Every day, my mother looked at me as if she had not told me this the day before and said, "Tiffany, you are so smart. You are so loved. You are so beautiful." By the time I was fifteen, it was pretty annoying. And I tell you, it's part of the reason why I am who I am. Growing up hearing every day you are beautiful, smart, and loved helps you walk into any room with a deep sense inside that you are enough, that you are worthy. When you have that belief in yourself, you tend to have a lot of faith in your decision-making, your intuitiveness, and your gut instincts. I got a jumpstart on developing my presence as a leader because every day my mother told me, "You're so smart, you're so loved, and you're beautiful."

This chapter opens with a quote from Tiffany's bestselling book *Drop the Ball: Achieving More by Doing Less*. She tells a story about a moment in her life when her mother backed her up without even needing to know all the details of an incident. While attempting to scale a fence one day, a neighborhood boy placed his hands up her dress. In a righteous rage, Tiffany got her hands on one of her father's tools and returned to the scene, swinging a hammer, which grazed the boy's head. His mother arrived soon after, angrily yelling at Tiffany's mother and demanding an apology for what happened, but they received no such apology. Instead, Tiffany's mother stood up for her daughter. It was an affirmation that standing up for herself would always be the right thing to do, even if it made others upset. Years later, when Tiffany started to feel she was losing control and losing her way, thinking about that incident brought her back to herself. Believing in yourself is the first key to developing a presence as a leader.[31]

Here's an exercise you might do when you are feeling unsure: write down three of the best decisions you've made in your life. Maybe it was leaving a toxic work environment or ending a relationship that wasn't healthy. Maybe it was moving to a new city, even though relocating was scary. Maybe it was a lifestyle change, like taking up a new sport or hobby. Write down just your top three decisions ever and reflect on how

---

31   Tiffany Dufu and Gloria Steinem, *Drop the Ball: Achieving More by Doing Less* (New York: Flatiron Books, 2018).

you knew what to. You are the same person who made those good choices, and you can still believe in yourself.

TRUST YOUR INTUITION

Lunch is a tough act to follow at conferences and events. Some people return from an afternoon meal feeling sleepy, while others don't return at all. Despite the Ellevate Network team's best effort, it was difficult to corral the sixty or so of us chapter leaders back to the presentation area in the spacious, modern loft where they had gathered all of their regional board members for a special training ahead of the organization's annual summit. I wasn't the only person who stared ahead, unsure of what to expect, because I noticed how others around me fidgeted in their chairs, making eye contact with each other, shrugging their shoulders, as if to say, *"Okay, here we go..."*

Before us stood Susan Mazonson, a petite, middle-aged woman wearing a well-tailored pantsuit, the kind we've grown accustomed to seeing Hillary Clinton wear. She had a head of perfect coils, a mix of brown and gray, and you could tell it was smoothed and gelled into submission. Next to her was a large easel and an oversized notepad with markers. On the other side of the easel stood Erica, a tall, lean woman with long blonde hair. She was a millennial, likely in her mid-thirties, and she was donning an eclectic Bohême chic attire. The visual contrast made me more curious.

Over the next hour and a half, they gave a masterclass on how to let the power of sharing and connecting through authentic stories lead us to discover more effective ways of leading in our careers and as volunteers. Susan and Erica, who later identified themselves as stepmother and stepdaughter, took turns telling the story of how they met and conveyed with great candor, humor, and care how they had gone from being coach and client to chosen family.

As they retold how experimenting, listening from within, being guided by intuition, and opening themselves up to intergenerational sharing changed the course of their lives, they invited us to turn a new page of our own, to start thinking differently about how our own relationships could bloom if watered by authenticity. Together, we filled many of those oversized white notepad pages with words representing ideas and visions of a way of working together as women to create communities that were richer and more welcoming.

Where Tiffany was preparing her entire life for a career committed to advancing women and received mentoring by women's movement leaders like Gloria Steinem who authored the foreword to her book, Susan would not have wanted to be anywhere near a room like this one thirty years ago, and maybe not even five years prior. The eldest of three siblings, as early as age four, she remembers being aware of the differences in how the boys and girls played.

All the action was with the boys, and she wanted in on that energy. She wasn't interested in playing it safe with the girls. She modeled herself after her dad. Susan was just fifteen when her father passed away suddenly, and she took over where he left off, becoming the pragmatic, reliable, stable energy her family needed. As a young woman, Susan made agreements with herself about how her life would go. She would ask no one for anything. She would make her own way. She would not be weak. These were things she would say to herself.

I was dismissive of the movements to advance women going on in the sixties and seventies. I thought I was above all of that. It felt like a distraction. Let other women burn their bras. I was going to need mine where I was going. I focused on power, and everything I did aligned with getting access to the spaces where men held power. Everything I've learned in my life has landed me in such a different place. I thought I was choosing to lead with masculine energy, but so much of my wiring and what made me successful came from my feminine energy and leadership qualities. These just weren't things we defined back then as powerful."

Susan pinpointed a moment of internal reckoning when, standing in what she describes as her "massive, beautiful, exquisite apartment"—which she had pieced together from acquiring several units in her building and renovating them over the years—she whispered to herself, wholly dissatisfied, "I'm done."

Her apartment would have been a dream in any city, but it was a feat, a near impossibility in New York City. With a view of Manhattan's Central Park from the west with seventeen windows, two floors, and a clear shot of all the landmark buildings, including the original Chippendale architecture of the original AT&T building, Susan could see just how far she had come. The recent graduate of Brown University walked into this residential building as a renter looking for an easy commute to her job, and now had the perspective of an accomplished businesswoman who had done mostly everything she had set on her mind. There she stood with a sense of emptiness where she expected to feel accomplished.

All the years of striving left her depleted, and she engaged a coach to help her reconnect with the pieces of herself she had left outside the boardrooms where she spent most of her time for almost three decades. This exploration led her to the midtown loft where we met and where she told her story for the first time.

It still takes my breath away thinking about the moment I realized my orientation all along was toward connectedness, truth, love, wisdom, and innovation. I learned all this by completing an assessment with my coach, and I was off the charts on those things. All those years, I was succeeding in a man's world. I was using my feminine superpowers. All the time I was winning big contracts, negotiating deals, and solving problems, it was my ability to connect, be honest, transparent, and to innovate that was showing up.

It doesn't seem like a coincidence to me the year Susan describes as one of her most lucrative, the one which put her company on a trajectory to sustained high earnings, she was pregnant with her daughter. Could it be the newfound love and maternal wisdom was helping her navigate the world differently? I think so. What I learned from Tiffany and Susan is our feminine intuition, our innate orientation, is there whether we choose to claim it or not. No two women are the same. Some women naturally exude more masculine qualities, and that's okay. Bea Arthur sums this up better than I could:

This is not about man-bashing. The problem isn't with mas-culine energy, it's with the imbalance. I'm half dude. We all are. I actually have a more masculine nature. I'm aggressive, ambitious, and all of that is masculine energy. Balance is good for everyone. I want to be successful and empowered, but I want better examples of men and women using their power. I love women who can do both—be great at business and also be vulnerable. Balance is building a great company, being present for their loved ones, and being honest about when it's hard and when you need help.

GET OUT OF YOUR OWN WAY

Nowadays, most people accept imposter syndrome is real, and anyone can experience this phenomenon. Let's talk about self-sabotage, though. Both of these things have a common root cause: fear. We have to be able to tell the dif-ference between the two and develop the appropriate tools for effectively handling these impediments to our success.

Whereas imposter syndrome tends to show up as we climb and feel more visible, vulnerable, and exposed, self-sabotage may be so debilitating it keeps us from ever even starting our ascent. It can look like procrastination, paralysis, or perfec-tionism. When it's never the right time, we never seem to commit, or nothing is ever quite good enough, and we need honestly examine if we are sabotaging ourselves. If we don't get out of our own way, we will never get anywhere.

It's important to remember our fear triggers won't always look like some big, daunting, external obstacle. Sometimes it presents as an internalized limiting belief, which has become an invisible security blanket keeping us from getting out and trying something new. In these moments, the monster we need to stare down and bring to its knees is within us.

This can be especially challenging because she will sometimes masquerade as our friend. She is what Tara Mohr, in her book *Playing Big: Practical Wisdom for Women Who Want to Speak Up, Create, and Lead*, calls our "inner critic." This voice, which can be both a menace and a nuisance, serves a valuable purpose. The problem is not that she exists but that she oversteps. It helps to remember that she is part of us, not the boss of us, and take back control. We have the power to turn the volume up or down on our internal dialogue. We can change the conversation at any time.[32]

The day I met Genevia Sawyer, she was showing an exhibit at the Naturalista Expo, which was held that year in Downtown Silver Spring at the Civic Center. This annual lifestyle convention was a go-to event for the DC, Maryland, and Virginia regions, drawing thousands of Black vendors, natural hair and beauty aficionados, and fashion and wellness bloggers. A mutual friend introduced us that afternoon at Genevia's booth, and we bonded instantly. We were two women who had recently launched new ventures.

It also helped that we have similar complexions and skincare needs. It's really difficult trying to explain undertones to non-black women at Sephora who have no real experience with how products behave on my skin, but I could trust Genevia's

---

32   Tara Mohr, *Playing Big: Find Your Voice, Your Mission, Your Message* (New York: Avery, 2015).

recommendations. Since high school, I've worn makeup daily, but I don't like to look overly made up. I'm all about enhancing, not erasing what I look like naturally. Her products were exactly what I had been missing—cruelty-free, eco-friendly, vegan, nontoxic nude lipsticks made with love for Black women of all hues. I was heartbroken when she stopped producing the 3:27 Cosmetics in summer 2020 to focus on the rapidly growing business consulting arm of her company, h.b Lighthouse.

What I didn't know the day we met was Genevia almost didn't get her company off the ground at all. One of the reasons natural beauty brand owners seek her out as a coach is because of how much she relates to their start-up struggles. She knows firsthand how paralyzing fear can be, and she can attest to the breakthroughs that follow once we get out of our own way.

The first time I was laid off from my job, my grandmother passed away that week. More than confused or hysterical, I was angry. I always imagined handing in my resignation letter before anyone could lay me off. I also lived in Brooklyn, New York, one of the most expensive cities in the country. What was I going to do with no job, bills that didn't care about my employment status, and a dream, which at the time, I felt was unattainable? I didn't have to wonder about that for very long, though, because I was hired back.

It may have seemed like the window of opportunity was gone, but another one soon opened up. This time, Genevia didn't hesitate.

The second time I got laid off from the same company, my disposition was different. I was relieved, annoyed, and liberated. Relieved because I hated my job. Annoyed because that morning, I had gotten out of my bed, hurried to get dressed, and commuted all the way to Manhattan just to be sent back home one hour later. Most importantly, I felt liberated because I could finally focus on being an entrepreneur. I realized the block all along had been me. My own fear was holding me back, and everything else was an excuse. About four months later, I officially launched.

This new makeup line was biographical, and the problem she was solving was personal. Having worked in the cosmetics industry as a copywriter and marketer, she knew all too well the way the industry spoke to women, the standards it upheld and imposed, and the many who were left out of the stories it told about beauty. She had personally found it difficult to find nude and matte lipsticks that complimented her complexion, and she was tired of being bombarded with products, many of them made with toxic ingredients. Mostly, she was fed up with normalizing the idea that beauty was unachievable while maintaining a natural look.

For four years, I had worked on 3:27 off and on, but I was inconsistent. There had always been a voice in my head telling me it wasn't the right time. But on that cold February day, walking back to my apartment unemployed, I decided to get out of my own head and out of my own way. There were no more excuses, just steady execution. I had no safety net to catch me, no nest egg of savings to get me through, so it wasn't my circumstances that had changed. I just decided to look at the situation differently—no more procrastination.

When I say to get out of your own way, I'm not advocating being quixotic. As a business consultant to start-up beauty brands focused on wellness and sustainability, I know Genevia wouldn't either. There's nothing glamorous about being broke. For some women who are the primary breadwinner or caretaker in a family, it would be harmful to jump into running a business prematurely. Getting out of our own way is about not becoming paralyzed by fear. If you are taking steps, however small or slow, toward accomplishing your goal, that's commendable.

Deborah Owens is the founder and CEO of WealthyU and a mentor to start-up founders with organizations like SEED SPOT and IFundWomen. As a financial advisor and coach, radio host, and best-selling author, she helps women leverage the power of the purse to build wealth and create lives of purpose. During a packed session at PurpleCON in 2019, she cautioned women against making snap decisions that could have long-term repercussions for themselves and their families. She rejects the idea all businesses have to start with venture capital or even financing and says instead, women should take the time to vet and validate their business ideas and focus on revenue.

There are many stories of founders who have emptied their bank accounts and retirement savings to pursue their dreams, but rarely do we hear the entire story. We don't know who their parents, grandparents, and spouses are. We only hear of the successes, but rarely the failures that ruined people's lives and futures. Women, especially, have no business putting themselves at financial risk for a business. If your business isn't making money within two years, then you don't have a business, and maybe you should consider getting a job and coming back to the idea when better prepared to execute it or moving on to a better idea.

Getting out of your own way does not mean losing touch with reality or blindly following what you have seen other people do without an honest analysis of your circumstances. So much of what we see on social media is fake. Lots of people are sharing only the highlight reels without being honest about all of the losses they are taking along the way. Rather than jumping quickly into the foray of entrepreneurship, it is better to be thoughtful and to take your time, weighing all the factors. Still, there comes a time to take the leap. There will never be the perfect set of circumstances, and there are no guarantees. Getting out of your own way means not letting fear hold you hostage and hold you back. We do that in big and small ways each day.

By developing our presence, listening to our intuition, and getting out of our own way, we can lead like the powerful women we are. By embracing our uniquely feminine leadership qualities, we position ourselves for success. Rather than trying to play the game of leadership by masculine rules, we instead play to our innate strengths.

CHAPTER 11:

KISS PERFECTIONISM GOODBYE

"In our culture, we make it feel like you're either a success or a failure—and that if you fail, that's it. But it's just not true. Everyone loves a comeback."

—SALLIE KRAWCHECK

The pursuit of perfection is a losing game, and I should know because I've been playing it most of my life. I still like to think I can help it, and one day I'll grow out of this tendency. I realize that's partly where the problem lies. Some personality traits are hardwired. We don't simply grow out of them, but we can grow through them. Just as I must accept my imperfection, I must also accept I might never shake the desire to be my best.

Nothing stirred my perfectionist impulses like becoming an entrepreneur, where I was confronted daily with all of my flaws and shortcomings. I'm no expert, but I have developed some helpful practices to make it easier for me to deal with my own failings and those of people around me. It feels like a long breakup, but I'm learning how to live without perfection, and you can too.

FORGIVE YOURSELF QUICKLY AND GENEROUSLY

The initial reflex of a recovering perfectionist after recognizing they've failed is to self-punish or want to find someone else to blame and then punish. I'm the foremost of offenders. It sometimes takes me days to recover from a minor blunder. I analyze every aspect of the decision or interaction. I rehash it with one of my friends or my husband or my mom. What's holding me back at those moments from moving on is my inability to forgive myself quickly, to be as generous with myself as I would be with anyone else.

The cost is a significant loss of time and energy, which translates to money, which I cannot afford. With support from my community, advisors, and coaches, I am learning to practice self-forgiveness as a tool to help me stay focused on the big picture and not all of the inevitable day-to-day failures. I give myself a reasonable amount of time to grieve the loss of face (because let's be real: it often comes down to embarrassment over feeling exposed). When my time is up, I pull it together and get back to work. My goal is to need less and less time for this recovery, but I'm a work in progress, and part of this is accepting my own messiness.

It's not always easy to recover from a setback, especially when the person we've let down the most is ourselves. Take my friend and client Danyelle Murray, for example. As an undergraduate at Hampton University, she majored in entrepreneurship and was known to have a few successful hustles as a bookseller and event promoter. When she was growing up, her dad owned his own business, and she always envisioned she would start her own company.

After a few of her initial ventures out of college didn't go as planned, she resigned herself to getting a job, and with each passing year, she became more down on herself for not having pursued her dreams. Almost a decade out of college, Danyelle was still holding on to an idea of what it was supposed to be like, and anything short of that perfect vision felt like a failure.

I started to feel real pressure about the future for the first time in my life after college. Even though I was an audacious youth who took risks and always tried new things, as an adult, I was afraid of getting things wrong, of not measuring up. Without realizing it, I began to shrink, and I fell in line with most of the people around me. I found a good job and told myself this was the responsible thing to do. Instead of immediately following my passion to become an entrepreneur, I let it go. But that didn't make me happy.

The truth is, Danyelle wasn't fair to herself. Perfectionism is inherently unfair. By being perfectionists, we hold ourselves to a standard that is impossible to reach with any amount of effort. Danyelle had to forgive herself and redirect all the energy she was using to condemn herself to create her dream business. We worked together over several months to brand her company The Audacity Lab, a strategic consulting agency that helps education, nonprofit, and philanthropic organizations unleash the power of youth voice, agency, and leadership to achieve breakthrough results. Along the way, those same perfectionist impulses would resurface. By allowing herself the freedom to experiment, to learn, and to grow through the feedback and input of others, things started to shift.

INVITE CRITIQUE OFTEN AND OPENLY

It's especially important for those of us attached to the delusion of our own exceptionalism to create room for others to burst our bubble from time to time. It is too easy to forget just because we show up brilliantly lots of the time doesn't mean we're not showing up poorly other times. Unfortunately, off-days and fumbles may make a lasting impression, which is difficult to reverse. Ultimately, we cannot control what anyone else thinks about us, and it is pointless to try. Still, it's necessary to be aware, reflective, and open to critique.

As entrepreneurs, we spend so much time in our own heads dreaming, planning, and imagining what's possible for the future we can sometimes lose sight of what is happening in the right now. There's real value in hearing from our team, our clients, our partners, and really anyone who experiences us on a regular basis. We need others to tell us the truth, and for that to happen, we need them to genuinely believe we want to hear it.

If someone you know and trust points out a character flaw or blind spot, then the wise thing to do would be to work on improving. Typically, it would be a family member, friend, coach, or colleague who might feel comfortable enough to be so direct. We all have unsavory personality traits, and people who care about us will want us to be better. If that feels personal, it's because it is. On the other hand, if someone points out a glitch in our client onboarding process or questions the efficacy or validity of our methods, it would be a mistake to confuse that feedback as an indictment of our character. It's not personal, and we shouldn't take it personally.

We want to avoid being tone-deaf, because no one is above criticism. Some of us make the mistake of trying to interpret or read into what others say, thinking we know what they *really* meant. We don't. We know what they said. My rule of thumb is to take what others say at face value and always with a grain of salt. Whenever I feel myself spiraling, I ask myself which voice is talking. Could it be my own internal self-talk I'm projecting onto what was said to me? Taking a few minutes to check in with myself, to reflect on where I'm feeling more or less confident often helps me to avoid taking any feedback too personally.

We often hear it said, "Beauty is in the eye of the beholder." Design is subjective, as Brandi Mebane, founder of social impact design firm Mebane Design Studio, knows well. It turns out, though, the iteration and experimentation going into producing web and digital products for clients provide a useful framework for growing her business. Letting go of perfectionism is critical to successfully delivering for clients, who are often demanding and dissatisfied the first go around. She's had to develop a thick skin, never taking critique too personally. More than that, Brandi has learned from experience the value of partnering with other designers to grow her business. This, too, requires being able to step back and approach these conversations with a level of objectivity and look for alignment as well as let go of thinking she can be and do all things.

It took four years of building her company to build steady revenue and be able to pay herself. Along the way, she also achieved brand recognition in greater Baltimore, becoming *radius rich*, a term that applies to people who have a heightened local profile. Getting to this point was arduous, and it required relinquishing power, trusting others, and being willing to hear their ideas and feedback. Enlisting feedback from advisors and staying open to making adjustments in her business model has been invaluable.

When I get tough feedback or start to doubt myself, I remember why I started. Celebrating entrepreneurship didn't happen when I was growing up. Everyone dismissed it as just a street hustle, and there was some skepticism of people who were entrepreneurs in my community—the people mocked for selling t-shirts out the back of their car. But I want young girls coming after me to see a viable path for starting their own companies and growing them. I'm doing all this to give people a platform for sharing their ideas with the world. That's what keeps me from getting too down on myself when the perfectionism starts flaring up.

Nowadays, it can be tough to pinpoint the exact first place you read a quote because there's content everywhere. Some time ago, a colleague posted on Instagram a quote that said, "If they don't know you personally, don't take their criticism personally." It seems worth saying that while everyone will have an opinion on what you should do, not everyone's opinion deserves your consideration. Sometimes the best way to subdue the perfectionism monster is not to feed her. Stay open, but also be discerning. Knowing when to shut off or shout out content or negative comments that make us doubt or distrust ourselves is critical to keeping our balance and staying energized.

LEARN FROM THE FAILURES OF OTHERS

If you're failing at something, you're probably not the first person or the last person to do so. We will all fail at some point, but some failures are absolutely preventable if we pay attention, ask the right questions, and take good advice. Before embarking on a new initiative, launching a new product, or exploring some new opportunity, do your research. Seek out others in your network and ask them what their most recent failures have been and what they've learned.

Marion Biglan is the founder and CEO of Illuminate Coaching, a leadership development and consulting practice that partners with executives and senior leadership teams to build their capacity as leaders and a culture where everyone has the safety and support to let their inner brilliance shine. She learned firsthand the power of learning from others' failures.

There was a time when I was afraid to see things about myself that were uncomfortable—my own whiteness, for example. From a young age, I had noticed differences in how some people were treated based on how they looked. I hadn't explored or confronted what it meant to be a white woman who benefited from the systems ascribing meaning to our differences

and ensuring some benefited while others were disadvantaged.
My defensive optimism created blinders, and as long as the
hard-to-look-at things stayed hidden, I felt safe. One day the
blinders were yanked away. A colleague called me out: 'You
just don't get it, Marion. And until you do, our organization
will never do right by our kids.' I wish I could say I took action
at that moment to understand better what I was missing, that
I reached out to my colleague to learn about his perspectives.

Marion understands how hard it can be to talk about failure, to admit where we could have done or could be doing better. She has also experienced the power of engaging with failure as an opportunity to learn and grow. When she was ready to do the work of improving her leadership, she sought support from a network of peers. Within these safe spaces, she could reflect, learn from leaders she respected who faced similar challenges, and stay accountable to herself and the change process. In her own coaching practice, there are many ways Marion partners with nonprofit, education, and social impact leaders, but she's most passionate about facilitating trainings for white leaders who are committed to building anti-racist organizations. She knows that sitting in this discomfort is not easy, and she harnesses her own experiences as a compassionate guide. For Marion, it's all about helping people shine the light on things that are uncomfortable to see and illuminate the path forward.

Nobody is perfect, and we should all give up trying to be. What are your blind spots? Where can you grow? Consider reaching out to someone who will share their own stories of failure and what they learned. Make it an intentional practice to ask peers and mentors what they are working to improve and how they are going about it. These conversations require earnestness, candor, and courage, and maybe even a bit more time. Consider them an investment in your long-term success. More than that, your humility and commitment to growth will leave an impression on others, and they will become (or stay) your champions, even when you fail.

When we let go of perfectionism, we free ourselves from the debilitating burden of expectations, and we open ourselves to new possibilities. Building a social enterprise is hard enough without us making it even more difficult. It's as simple as this: kiss perfection goodbye and say hello to greater joy and satisfaction as an entrepreneur.

CHAPTER 12:

BE MISSION-DRIVEN, BUT NOT A MARTYR

———

"Success is liking yourself, liking what you do, and liking how you do it."

—MAYA ANGELOU

When you are a mission-driven entrepreneur, your heart's involvement is on a much deeper level than when building a business for financial profit alone. If you succeed, you don't only enrich yourself, you also help change the lives of others. All of this can be weighty. This chapter is written from a particularly vulnerable place because I am just as guilty as the next woman of martyring myself for a cause. It can be difficult to separate a mission from a ministry.

Many of us pursue entrepreneurship because we have discovered our passion. It's the thing we would do or talk about all day for free. Some people say once you've found your passion, work won't feel like work anymore. While that's a nice sentiment, many later find that to be untrue. If you find the thing you love to do so much you will do it for free, you have a hobby. Once you make that hobby a hustle, you no longer have the option of doing it for free, and if you don't adjust that thinking, you may end up hating the thing you once loved. Resistance to this may show up as a hesitation to stand up for yourself in contract negotiation or a reluctance to raise your rates.

Too many women I've spoken with have lamented being caught in a vicious cycle of overworking, overcommitting, and overproducing while enjoying few-to-no rewards for their labors. The pattern among Black and Latinx founders was they were expected to work harder, better, smarter, and were also expected to be grateful and gracious, even in the face of grossly unfair compensation and chronic underinvestment in their ventures. We're not going to recount all that makes the playing field uneven. What we will focus on now is how to shift our mindset.

What disturbed me most in listening to women's stories was the extent to which so many of us had internalized the unfair expectations. We were now the unreasonable taskmasters applying an inordinate amount of pressure. We had learned to navigate the oppressive structures so well we were doing an even better job than any boss of keeping ourselves in line. We didn't impose these roles, but we have enforced them because too few of us have experienced anything else. From the time we're kids, we learn to work twice as hard and not expect the same recognition or reward, but that's just not sustainable.

By opening up a dialogue about this, I'm inviting anyone who supports, partners, and invests in women of color to gain a deeper understanding of what we experience. With this insight, you can be more intentional about eliminating barriers than constructing artificial ones, even unintentionally. It starts, I believe, with how women of color see themselves, but it can't end there. We all have a part to play in transforming how we work. As I listened to women who are leading mission-driven organizations explain how they managed to stay true to their cause without becoming a martyr for it, a few themes emerged, and I'm sharing their loving invitations to be better to ourselves.

DEFINE SUCCESS ON YOUR OWN TERMS

Imagine how empowering it must have felt for Kathryn Finney to put fingers to the keyboard and hit publish on a *Medium* article dated May 22, 2020, entitled, "I Built It. And Now I'm Moving On." Finney built the nonprofit organization digitalundivided, which for a decade helped usher in the next cadre of Black women tech founders—providing a launching pad for their ideas and a megaphone for them to become known. Along the way, she discovered that while it was great to identify talented Black female entrepreneurs and introduce them to the world, it wasn't enough if investors weren't ready or willing to get behind them.

At the onset of the global coronavirus pandemic, as thousands of businesses were closing and women and people of color were experiencing a conflation of devastating losses, Finney decided to be part of the solution. She incubated the Doonie Fund, named after her own grandmother, who was a successful entrepreneur. Within weeks, she deployed thousands of dollars of microgrants, which served as lifelines for Black women-owned businesses. She learned two things, two truths she had intuited all along as she reflected on her challenges raising money, despite having all the receipts: "1. Black women are amazing money managers, and 2. People don't trust Black women with money." She was moving on to grow the Doonie Fund and to solve the real problem in investment, which was that there weren't enough investors willing to bet on Black women.

The people who fund things—whether it's a venture capitalist or a philanthropist—are often those who have benefited directly from the inequities in our society. This is why they have money in the first place. As Anand Giridharadas explains in his book Winners Take All, these are people who want "to change the world while also profiting from the status quo," and the status quo is women, especially Black women, remaining essential workers, but not essential owners. There's a visceral reaction that happens when you're a Black woman, and you declare your worth. I've had people recoil when I asserted my value in a negotiation. As in, "How dare you?" When a Black woman is clear on her worth or chooses herself, others view it as offensive. Because, as a Black woman, you should sacrifice your economic stability, your health, and your sanity for everyone else. You don't even get to own your sanity.

Less than 2 percent of venture capital investment goes to women, and only a fraction of that funding goes to Black women. We still have a long way to close the gaps for more traditional business financing along gender and racial lines. This fact is complicated by assumptions made about how fundraising should happen, with most angel investors and venture capitalists assuming funders should start by asking their friends and family.

Before Cheryl Contee cofounded the digital design company Do Big Things, she made history in 2012 when her company Attentive.ly, a tech start-up specializing in influencer marketing and digital fundraising, was acquired by Blackbaud, making it the first tech start-up with a Black female founder on the board to be acquired by a NASDAQ-traded company. She talks about the conundrum of the "friends and family round" and the other barriers women, diverse, and first-generation founders in technology start-ups face in her book *Mechanical Bull: How to Achieve Startup Success*.

For the nontraditional, minority, or female founder, you may already be one of the most successful people in your family with few more experienced nearby models on which to tap. Your family and friends are trying to borrow money from you, not the other way around!

Because building a venture requires support from a broad community, and there are so many unstated norms to follow, we sometimes forget we still set the terms. We must remember we determine our own destiny; no one else is empowering it. We decide what's nonnegotiable. As founders, we start with a clear vision, and people invest in us because we compel them. If we can convince them to follow our lead once, we can do it again. The key is to maintain an unwavering belief in ourselves and to refuse to let anyone else determine our value for us. When you can no longer speak with the same conviction, then you owe it to yourself and everyone who supports you to move on.

Sometimes that's the best thing. Maybe you've accomplished your part, and it's time to let someone else take over and bring it to the next level. Or maybe you've discovered along the way the root cause of the problem you're hoping to solve and can address it through a different means. Possibly you've hit a wall, and it would require compromising a fundamental value to keep going.

Being mission-driven means staying focused on the destination, not the vehicle. If you were on a road-trip in a rental car and it broke down, wouldn't you be open to switching cars so you could keep going? Or would you cancel the whole trip if you couldn't continue in the car with which you started? Most reasonable people would regroup and keep going because getting to their destination is what matters. Sure, it would be disruptive, and it may even set you back a few hours, but it would be worth it to persevere. Knowing when to walk away is just as important as knowing how to keep pushing. You determine what success looks like for you, not anyone else.

DRAW STRENGTH FROM YOUR COMMUNITY

Women who have long been undervalued and overlooked at work are finding financial freedom and growth opportunities through what has been dubbed *necessity entrepreneurship*. I'm not in love with the term itself, but the concept speaks to something that too often goes unnamed. In recent years, we have seen the rise of popular movements where women have come forward with the stories of the abuses they have sustained while trying to make a living. More often than not, the women whose stories have received the most attention have been rich, powerful, famous, and white. Either that or the perpetrators of the abuses have been, which made it newsworthy. Still, what used to be relegated to hushed conversations among friends and coworkers has finally gone mainstream.

We have already established that women, particularly women of color, are fighting for access to capital and are starting companies at higher rates. Among the myriad reasons, I suspect it has something to do with a deep frustration with playing a game that is rigged against us. Instead of fighting for a seat at tables where they aren't welcome, many are building their own board rooms. It seems there has been a collective awakening to the necessity of rebuilding the future workplace in radically different ways. The scrappy ingenuity that has fueled industry and innovation throughout the modern era is taking on a new shape in this current time. Undoubtedly, this results from a combination of factors, but what's undeniable is that a generation of women whose talent, connectedness, and level of educational attainment has never been higher will not settle indefinitely for the grossly unfair and exclusionary practices.

Take, for example, Doris Quintanilla, founder and CEO of The Melanin Collective. A proud Latinx, first-generation, and disabled entrepreneur, Doris is on a mission to promote healing across the nonprofit sector and help people and organizations reach new heights as a result. For her, the professional became personal after sustaining a head injury at work that changed her life and career trajectory. Doris is no stranger to hard work. As the daughter of immigrants, she grew up watching members of her family and community work tirelessly to achieve the American Dream. She was a diligent student who worked hard to become the first person in her family to attend a highly selective college.

She could feel the burnout approaching in the weeks before she traveled to Mexico for a two-week training, but she ignored it. There was no time to honor what her body needed. Her nonprofit job was very demanding, and she felt fortunate to be working for an organization where she could do work that mattered. She boarded an international flight to meet her colleagues in the field and never let the exhaustion show. But during a team-building excursion on the last day of the trip, she hit her head. To this day, the details around her injury are fuzzy. She doesn't remember much of anything about the accident itself, but she can't forget the excruciating headaches, sleepiness, or slurred speech, because these things are still with her, even after years of therapy. Everyone on her team, including her boss, saw her accident, but no one took her to the hospital or made sure she was okay.

Within a week of returning from the trip, her mom noticed something was very wrong and urged her to get checked out. Unbeknownst to her, the injury had caused internal bleeding in her brain, and the blood was collecting under her eyes. She required serious and immediate help. While she was trying to heal, things were picking up at work. Doris was promoted to a new role with a bigger title and more responsibility, but not given any salary increase. When her doctor insisted that she take short-term leave to focus on recovery or risk permanent brain damage, her company denied the claim and then fired her. It would be two years before she would successfully win her case against them.

During that time, Doris thought long and hard about what she wanted to do next. Prior to her accident, she was a top performer and trusted member of the team, leading many complex projects. After her accident, she was treated as disposable. As someone who developed a heart for community service as a little girl watching her dad lead a local nonprofit, she never expected this kind of treatment could be possible in an organization that was supposed to help people. When she thought about it, it wasn't just this one organization. She had been subjected to toxic stress in all of her previous nonprofit jobs too. What was that about?

I was broken, both physically and mentally. I was so tired of fighting them. The way I saw it, I had two options: Go make money in the private sector and forget all of this social impact stuff or start to understand how I could get to a place of healing and, in the process, heal the industry that broke my heart.

Doris initially felt angry and defeated, but then something happened. She started talking to others about her experiences. She realized she wasn't alone. In time, she started The Melanin Collective. Initially, the group came together for commiseration. What they all shared in common was that they were women of color recovering from the trauma of working in nonprofits. They needed a safe space where they could speak openly, have their experiences validated, and plan for the future. The Melanin Collective emerged as an organization for women of color to have courageous and cathartic conversations that other people were too afraid to have. Eventually, Doris grew the organization into a consulting practice that advises nonprofit executive teams and organizational leaders in transforming their workplace cultures. She leverages the power of her story to advocate for others and often helps coach professionals out of their jobs in toxic organizations.

Many well-intentioned people are doing more harm to the communities they serve and the people they claim to support. It's because these folks haven't done their own healing. Even three years ago, it was still taboo to talk about racism, and white supremacy was showing up in the social impact sector. Everyone told me I was being too brazen, too vocal. But talking the way I did led me to my people. I attracted my community and the right clients. My company and all of my consultants are thriving, and it's because we were unapologetic.

Your community is out there, and they are looking for you. Never forget the power of your story and the healing that comes from telling it to others. This is how you will draw strength to pursue your purpose, even after a setback.

TAKE GOOD CARE OF YOURSELF— NOT JUST ON SUNDAYS

Self-care is about so much more than bubble baths and deep tissue massages, even though both are amazing and sometimes exactly what we need. Taking good care of ourselves is a daily commitment to meeting our most basic human needs physically, mentally, emotionally, and spiritually so we can sustain ourselves. Eating good food, drinking enough water, and getting adequate rest are not suggestions. These are instructions for how to operate our bodies, and when we ignore requirements, we cause damage. The difference between being mission-driven and a martyr is about balance. When we push too far beyond our limits, that's when it becomes dangerous.

Everyone should take good care of themselves, but it's especially critical for women of color who have heightened risk factors to consider. Dr. Kumba Hinds Murray is a family physician and public health expert whose research published during her graduate tenure at the Yale School of Public Health explored correlations between race and women's physiology.

The association between stress and chronic disease is irrefutable. It's easy to imagine how stress is associated with mental health conditions like depression, but numerous studies show an association between stress and conditions like asthma and diabetes as well. Black women experience unique stress by being both female and Black and, not surprisingly, are disproportionately affected by chronic disease, cancers, COVID, maternal mortality—the list is endless.

Dr. Hinds Murray pointed out this heightened risk has less to do with genetics and correlates more to environmental factors. Black women's genetic code is nearly identical to other racial groups, and yet they are at higher risk. This is the case even when we account for socioeconomic status, education, income, and access to healthcare. This leads to only one plausible explanation: being a Black woman brings a higher level of toxic stress, which affects the mind and body. Since being an entrepreneur comes with its own unique stress, staying vigilant about self-care, especially for founders of color, is a matter of survival.

We cannot be of service to anyone if we're dead, but this is about more than staying alive. Too often, we overlook all the other dimensions of our personhood that also require care. I would argue not shrinking ourselves to fit the mold of inhospitable environments is a radical act of self-preservation. I remember a story Nita Baum tells about her mother. She resisted pressure from colleagues and superiors to trade in her Indian saris for American clothing in order to advance. Shutting out the voices around her, she listened instead to her own internal voice, and this lesson has helped Nita do the same as a founder.

By the time she retired, still wearing saris, my mom was revered for her scientific mastery and was a highly respected expert in her field. I often wonder, "How often do we abdicate our own power by separating from and abandoning ourselves? By seeking externally what we already have and can give to ourselves? What power arises within, and how do we navigate our relationships when we embody ourselves through trust, responsibility, and leadership? How much more connected are we when we are in our power?" The more we align our words and our actions to our inner knowing, the greater our trust and acceptance become. Power then arises more easily and from being in your flow rather than from force.

Rest is underrated. Sure, we need to sleep regularly to restore our strength and function, but it's even deeper than that. Years of grinding can take a toll on our spirit and steal our joy. Sometimes we need a longer break, a sabbatical. This can feel so foreign, especially to those of us who did not grow up knowing anyone who had the financial security to stop working for a period of time. Even if taking a sabbatical is a luxury you cannot afford in the present moment, consider planning for it in the future.

Halleemah Nash has made me a believer. In the midst of a pandemic and a moment of extreme uncertainty, she decided to launch a new company called Rosecrans Ventures. If that wasn't daring enough, she took a two-month sabbatical before going to work for herself full-time. When I asked her how she knew she needed this break and what convinced her to take the time she needed, she said it started with separating her value from her productivity.

I have had a job since I was fourteen, and I've always been proud of my ability to take care of myself and others. I feel valuable when accomplishing my goals. I feel valuable when my hands are working. But when I thought about my purpose in this world, I knew it had to be deeper than the works of my hands because there's a human behind these hands. As my mentor says, "We are human beings and not human doings."

Where had she learned to derive her value from laboring rather than being?

If I'm honest, that's the manual our mothers and our grandmothers pass down to us as Black women, not a manual for self-care but instructions for how to take care of the village. And I've learned it well. The pandemic created so much disruption in the communities where I work. Every time one of my students lost an internship, I believed it was my job to find them another one. Every time a parent called with a concern, I believed it was my job to help them find a solution.

There were signs she needed to slow down. She wasn't eating well or sleeping enough, and she was putting in fourteen-hour days. But it took something drastic. Everything came to a screeching halt after the elimination of her full-time position.

For over a year, I had been laying the foundation for my company, so I knew what I wanted to do next. My coach has been nudging me to take a sabbatical for a while, but I honestly dismissed it as something only rich white people did. That right there was the problem. I decided to do it to show Black girls they needed and deserved rest too. I documented my sabbatical and shared it on social media so the young people I mentor and who follow me would see more than just me grinding. It's not all about accomplishments. It's not all about the hustle.

PROTECT YOUR PEACE OF MIND AT ALL COSTS

"Sticks and stones may break my bones, but words will never hurt me." So the child's taunt goes, only we all know it's not true. We have all been injured at one point or another by someone else's unkind words. Early-stage founders, in particular, are often encouraged to network, and this can involve lots of formal and informal meetings with potential advisors, partners, investors, and clients. We are also encouraged to be coachable, open to feedback, and willing to learn from and incorporate the experiences and perspectives. This is all good, except men and women receive very different kinds of feedback, and women and people of color contend with implicit bias.

What we often hear in these conversations is less constructive criticism and more so character assassination. It's true all founders will get tough feedback at some point, and it is important to have tough skin, but some of what we contend with is inexplicable and inexcusable. The brilliant and effervescent Janice Omadeke is the founder and CEO of The Mentor Method. This technology platform helps companies create more inclusive and high-performing workplaces through the power of more intentional mentoring relationships.

She describes a moment that should be unbelievable, except that it's true.

I was at this networking breakfast seated at a round table with about ten other people, mostly other early-stage entrepreneurs. We were each meant to go around and share one pain point and make an ask of the others. I shared that as a first-generation American, my network is not robust enough for me to start with a friends and family round to fundraise for my company since most of my friends and family are making the equivalent of two dollars a day in the Congo. A well-known entrepreneur, someone I thought was friendly toward me, someone I had previously met with over coffee, responded, 'Well, maybe you should have spent less time in college with people who don't look and smell just like you.' I'm quick on my feet, so I made a joke of it and fired back with, 'If everybody smelled like Chanel No. 5, the world would be a much better place,' but it really hurt my feelings.

Janice admitted she lost valuable time for the rest of the day replaying that exchange. It wasn't that she didn't know there would be people who might say ignorant and cutting things, but she simply hadn't expected it. She recovered, and she has built an incredible company. What her story illuminated for me was why and with what vigilance we must protect our peace of mind. After this verbal attack, Janice gave herself a day to feel bad, and then she got back to work, and I think that's important to note.

Not everyone is willing to make room at the table, physically or proverbially, for women and diverse founders. It's still a battle against centuries of social conditioning not to see them as equals. Being confronted with blatant discrimination and bias is uncomfortable. Fixating on it or allowing it to shift our sense of self is a trap. Even though we know that we're human, we may have to give ourselves time to acknowledge our feelings before we move on.

Here it helps to have options, and one way to give ourselves the power to choose our destiny is to plan. I spoke to Melanie Rivera about the concept of self-authorship, the ability to retain full editorial rights over our lives and not to be forced into false choices. She believes a woman must always prepare for the moment when she will have to walk away to keep her sanity.

Having a 'forget you fund' is a powerful thing, especially for women and women of color in leadership. It is important to have the power to walk away from toxic and damaging situations, and that often looks like having at least six months' savings and knowing if you get fired or quit, you'll be okay. And they knew they'd be okay. They knew they'd be able to find another job. I think this is something that takes the edge off as a founder.

Walking away is much easier said than done. When you're doing work that feels like your life's calling, it can be easy to become so attached to your vision of success you forget there is more than one way to achieve your goals. Walking away from a situation that no longer serves you, even if it means starting over again, is not a failure. The failure would be to compromise your mental, emotional, and physical health.

I've taken to heart at some of my low moments this reminder from Cheryl Contee, who concludes her book with the thought:

No matter what happens, being an entrepreneur, you've already succeeded. Just by seeing yourself in that context of, "I have a great idea, and I believe I can be a leader and bring something into the world," you have already been successful. Your momma is already proud of you. That's the good news. [1]

One of the myths too many buy into is we're strong enough to persist despite all odds, and walking away to protect one's peace is weak. Bea Arthur makes a case for redefining what it means to be strong, especially as a Black woman founder. Where strong has sometimes meant keeping everything inside, putting on a smile for the outside world, and suffering in silence, she believes the key to strength and resilience is confronting our painful experiences and enlisting the support of a professional to help us develop coping strategies.

When my company was going through a difficult time, and I just knew it was going to fail, I called the suicide hotline four times. I have no shame admitting that. It's why I'm so determined to make mental health services accessible to everyone.

Within the entrepreneur community, anxiety, depression, addiction are all so high because it's such a brutal mental experience, and no business is worth your soul. Being your own boss is not worth your marriage or your mortgage. It's not okay to give it all you got and sacrifice at all costs because, more often than not, it's not going to work out. Companies fail all the time, and you need to know you're going to be okay regardless of what happens.

More than a mechanism for releasing the burdens we're often carrying, I have found working with a therapist or wellness coach has helped me develop my capacity to be a reflective and responsive leader, people manager, and decision-maker. Quite often, the justification for not seeking out professional services is they're too expensive. But how much is your peace of mind worth to you? Never forget you are the visionary. You can always pursue a new idea or build a new company or organization, but there is only one you.

CONTROL YOUR OWN NARRATIVE

You are the CEO of your own life. You are your own chief brand officer. You control your own narrative. Your story is the only thing you own and over which you have full creative control. Your story is not what happens to you; it's what happens next. It is not your circumstances; it is what you make of them.

When you are not intentional about the telling of your own story, someone else will tell it for you, and they will get it wrong. Don't abdicate your power. You are the rightful owner of your story. To own our story, we must first take control of our thoughts. The stories we tell ourselves about ourselves can help us combat the stories the society may tell about who we are and what we're capable of doing or being.

America Ferrera may be best known for her breakout performance in the sitcom *Ugly Betty* and as the first and only Latinx actress to ever win an Emmy in a lead category. In her TEDx Talk, she says, "My identity is a superpower—not an obstacle," as she traces her journey to self-acceptance. Not surprisingly, it didn't come as a result of accolades or commercial success.

I couldn't change what a system believed about me while I believed what the system believed about me. It is possible to be the person who genuinely wants to see change while also being the person whose actions keep things the way they are.

Sometimes the stories we tell ourselves and about ourselves are all we have. It can feel like an uphill battle to sit in rooms where we receive scrutinizing. This was something Halleemah recognized she needed to heal from during her sabbatical. Years of fighting to be respected had taken a toll on her, and when we talked about it, the pain was still palpable.

Being so different than everybody else at most of the tables where I've sat throughout my career has not only made me question my qualifications but question who I am as a person. It took me a very long time to see value in my differences, to realize I'm not only qualified to have a seat but to run this table. I spent time and energy fighting not to allow these systems to destroy me, not to allow my thought process and inner dialogue to destroy me.

One way to reclaim our narrative is to talk more about our accomplishments and the people who are behind these good things. It starts by sharing the real stories of women, many of whom are founders of color, who are changing the face of social entrepreneurship and achieving things previously thought unimaginable.

Maureen Murat, Esq. is the founder and CEO of Crowdie Advisors, an equity crowdfunding platform helping start-up founders with scalable businesses get access to funding in exchange for giving up some of the equity or ownership in their companies. She is ready for us to move on in the narrative we tell about women, and especially Black women, when it comes to access to funding and growth, and she sees a bright future ahead.

I think we focus a lot on how little funding women get, and we hear a lot about how hard it is to get venture capital investment. What we aren't talking about enough is the billions of dollars women and people of color are bringing in each year in sales. We are finding a way to make money with VCs, and that matters. It speaks to our resilience and our awesomeness, and that's where my passion lies. We need to redirect the focus to where we are successful if we want to see more of it.

We have a choice. We can kill ourselves trying to play by rules designed for us to fail, or we can rewrite the rules. We can choose to see ourselves as infinitely capable, brilliant, and equal to the challenges we'll face, or we can allow others to control our narrative. It's true, failures, setbacks, and missteps will happen along the way. Even then, we have a choice. We could build a case against our worthiness, our preparedness, our likelihood of success, or we can recast negative experiences as learnings. Many people will attempt to talk us out of our dreams, to impose upon us the limiting beliefs they have internalized about what's possible. We don't have to believe them. We are what we believe we are. Being in service of our mission doesn't mean martyring ourselves for the cause. Take good care of yourselves. You are needed.

CONCLUSION:

DARE LIKE NEVER BEFORE

———

It took me more than two weeks to go through the boxes because of exhaustion. I can't remember any other time in my adult life when I felt this burnout. I'm not sure of the exact day because, except for paying outstanding invoices to vendors and managing the return of video equipment from my interns, I hadn't moved much since I carried the last box up from the car and collapsed onto my bed.

I do know it was April 2019, and two weeks prior, I had pulled off what was easily one of the most significant events of my professional career to date: PurpleCON. I produced, curated, and mostly funded this two-day conference for women and diverse social entrepreneurs. The event featured nearly forty speakers and presenters from across the country and almost two-hundred attendees. Everyone who took the stage was amazing, and that's what people said in their surveys. I wasn't surprised by the glowing reviews of presenters because I personally researched, screened, and invited each one. Our attendees were also impressive in their accomplishments and their diversity. So many people I admired and adored descended on Washington, DC for those two days, and I should have been excited and really proud, but I wasn't. I was tired the entire time. The smile on my face, the pep in my step, and the enthusiasm in my voice all forced. Only nobody knew but me.

After everything was over and it was time to clear out the venue. I worked alongside the volunteer crew and the really amazing logistics team, who had pulled off the most impressive setups on a skeletal budget. I felt immense gratitude to each and every human who lingered with me that evening to ensure everything was carefully packed up, sent home with the appropriate person, or disposed of responsibly. My gratitude helped me hold it together. I even managed to grab dinner with a few close friends who insisted on celebrating me, but sometime before dessert came, I excused myself to the restroom, and I bawled.

Days later, I finally brought myself to sort through what remained from the conference so I could put things away in storage when the tears started flowing again. I couldn't believe my conference didn't make any money. I felt cheated, thinking all I would have to show for months and months of planning were purple lanyards, program books, gift bags, and posters I would probably have to throw out. The conference theme in 2019 was "Dare to Think Purple." As I sat sifting through paraphernalia with those bold words plastered across, I decided this was a moment when I could choose to drink my own purple Kool-Aid or give up and never show my face again.

It's obvious which path I chose, though at that moment, how I would put the pieces back together felt like a mystery. Some days later, I knew what I needed to do. I started working on this book and planning the next conference. Ultimately, "Rona"—the personification of this crazy pandemic that has brought the world to its knees—made it impossible for me to move forward with the large-scale event I had planned for late spring 2020. But she hasn't stopped me from sharing this book with you at exactly the right time.

In the year it took me to write this book, the globe has undergone massive disruption. A pandemic has caused health, financial, educational, and social-emotional crisis, unlike anything my generation has ever seen. It's not hyperbolic to state we literally have no idea how we'll get through this period or what the world will look like on the other side. What we need more than ever are people who "Dare to Think Purple." From the start, I've defined this thinking as creative, courageous, and confident thinking—a way of seeing the world through the lens of our shared humanity and looking through our stories to find solutions to the stickiest problems.

Most of my peers are equal parts mystified and petrified about the future of their social enterprises. Even those whose companies are doing well are operating in the same uncertain environment, breathing the same air, facing the same health threats. I'm convinced thriving in this period will require daring as we've never seen before. If you read to the end of this book and don't feel like you've learned anything particularly new, that's great. It means you recognize you had the answers all along. Hopefully, reading the stories of other women who are building something meaningful affirmed your belief in yourself and let you know you're not alone.

This book should read like a conversation with me and dozens of other women who are just like you, who know what you're going through. It's not easy. Getting to year five, while a significant achievement and a strong indication your business is viable and successful, comes with no guarantee things will get easier. The worries, the pressures, and the problems in your business will transform, change shape and color, but they'll still be there. For those of us who cannot help but build and create, we welcome it all. We want to know how to weather the storms, and this book should give you a peek into the journeys of women who have done so successfully. If you feel more inspired and encouraged as you press forward, then I have done my job.

I'll leave with one parting thought:

In the moments where we feel the greatest fear, there are also the greatest opportunities to be daring. We've reflected on the experiences of many other women over these many pages, and you've had a chance to step into each of their shoes. But take a moment now to just be present with yourself. Think about what success looks like for you. How will you be different? How will you change the lives of the people you love? What will become possible for others as a result of your endeavors? How will the world be better for your efforts? Whenever it feels tempting to stop, to shrink, or to second-guess, remember you have another option. You can "Dare to Think Purple."

So why are you waiting? Go change the world.

I dare you.

APPENDIX

———

INTRODUCTION—DARE TO THINK PURPLE

- Deane, Michael T. 2020. "Top 6 Reasons New Businesses Fail." *Investopedia.* February 28, 2020. https://www.investopedia. com/financial-edge/1010/top-6-reasons-new-businesses-fail. aspx#:~:text=Data%20from%20the%20BLS%20shows.

- Guerra, Maria. 2013. "Fact Sheet: The State of African American Women in the United States." *Center for American Progress,* November 7, 2013. https://www.americanprogress.org/issues/ race/reports/2013/11/07/79165/fact-sheet-the-state-of-african- american-women-in-the-united-states/

- Online Etymology Dictionary, *s.v.* "Dare." Accessed August 29, 2020. https://www.etymonline.com/word/dare.

CHAPTER 1—BE CLEAR

- Ingram, Heather C. *Applied Flow: Stop Burnout. Be Awesome.* New Degree Press, 2020.

- Molina Niño, Nathalie and Sara Grace. 2018. *Leapfrog: The New Revolution for Women Entrepreneurs*. New York: Tarcher-Perigee.

CHAPTER 2—BE CONFIDENT

- Kay, Katty, and Claire Shipman. *The Confidence Gap: The Science and Art of Self-Assurance—What Women Should Know*. New York: HarperCollins Publishers, 2014.

- Mohr, Tara. *Playing Big: Find Your Voice, Your Mission, Your Message*. New York: Avery, An Imprint of Penguin Random House. 2015.

- Saujani, Reshma. *Brave, Not Perfect: Fear Less, Fail More, and Live Bolder*. Penguin Random House Audio Publishing Group. 2019.

- *The Atlantic*. 2017. "Why Do Men Assume They're So Great?' *YouTube* video. https://www.youtube.com/watch?v=aiC3mu-5jWmY#action=share.

CHAPTER 3—BE CREATIVE

CHAPTER 4—BE COURAGEOUS

- Bell, Lisa Nicole, host. "Mandela SH Dixon on Reinventing Herself and Flipping Failure into Success." Behind the Brilliance (podcast). April 4, 2019. Accessed October 5, 2020. https://podcasts.apple.com/us/podcast/mandela-sh-dixon-on-reinventing-herself-flipping-failure/id859413671?i=1000434124135

- Bornstein, David. *How to Change the World: Social Entrepreneurs and the Power of New Ideas.* New York: Oxford University Press. 2007.

- Kiss, Melissa. "Courage–A Matter of The Heart." *Thrive Global,* March 29, 2018, https://thriveglobal.com/stories/courage-a-matter-of-the-heart/#:~:text=The%20root%20of%20the%20word. Accessed September 27, 2020.

CHAPTER 5—BUILD COMMUNITY

- Maddie, Sofia, host. "Your Brain on Storytelling." Short Wave (podcast). January 14, 2020. Accessed October 15, 2020. https://www.npr.org/2020/01/13/795977814/your-brain-on-storytelling

- Norwood, Tiffany Ann. *Vote Like a Boss: An Entrepreneur's Perspective on Innovation, Leadership, Creativity, Storytelling, and Voting.* Tribetan Press, 2020.

- Stengel, Geri. "A Black Women Entrepreneur Only Gets Funding Crumbs." *Forbes,* May 3, 2017. https://www.forbes.com/sites/geristengel/2017/05/03/the-next-steve-jobs-a-black-woman-only-gets-funding-crumbs/#5eff61a23c33. Accessed October 26, 2020.

CHAPTER 6—ACKNOWLEDGE THE PLAYING FIELD IS UNEVEN

- DuBow, Wendy, and Allison-Scott Pruitt. "The Comprehensive Case for Investing More VC Money in Women-Led Startups." *Harvard Business Review,* September 18, 2017. https://hbr.org/2017/09/the-comprehensive-case-for-investing-more-vc-money-in-women-led-startups?registration=success. Accessed July 22, 2020.

- Glynn, Sara Jayne. "Breadwinning Mothers Continue to Be the US Norm." Center for American Progress, June 10, 2005. https://www.americanprogress.org/issues/women/reports/2019/05/10/469739/breadwinning-mothers-continue-u-s-norm/. Accessed September 25, 2020.

- Hassan, Kamal, Monisha Varadan, and Claudia Zeisberger. 2020. "How the VC Pitch Process Is Failing Female Entrepreneurs." *Harvard Business Review.* January 13, 2020. https://hbr.org/2020/01/how-the-vc-pitch-process-is-failing-female-entrepreneurs.

- Kapin, Allyson. 2019. "10 Stats That Build the Case for Investing in Women-Led Startups." *Forbes,* January 28, 2019. https://www.forbes.com/sites/allysonkapin/2019/01/28/10-stats-that-build-the-case-for-investing-in-women-led-startups/#26d7f-27c59d5.

- "Population, Female (% of Total) Data." 2017. The World Bank, September 4, 2020. https://data.worldbank.org/indicator/SP.POP.TOTL.FE.ZS.

CHAPTER 7—TALK ABOUT THE TABOO STUFF

- Balassone, Cheryl. "Femly Founder Arion Long Is Changing Feminine Care. Period." *I95 Business*, December 10, 2018. https://i95business.com/articles/content/femly-founder-arion-long-is-changing-feminine-care-period-704. Accessed September 10, 2020.

- Krasny, Jill. 2012. "Infographic: Women Control the Money in America." *Business Insider.* February 17, 2012. https://www.businessinsider.com/infographic-women-control-the-money-in-america-2012-2#ixzz1mtTRybbl.

- Light, Paulette. 2013. "Why 43% of Women with Children Leave Their Jobs, and How to Get Them Back." *The Atlantic*, April 19, 2013. https://www.theatlantic.com/sexes/archive/2013/04/why-43-of-women-with-children-leave-their-jobs-and-how-to-get-them-back/275134/.

- Rueckert, Phineas. 2018. "Why Periods Are Keeping Girls Out of School & How You Can Help." Global Citizen, June 30, 2018. https://www.globalcitizen.org/en/content/menstrual-hygiene-day-education/#:~:text=Without%20access%20to%20proper%20education,drop%20out%20of%20school%20completely.

- Tory Burch Foundation. 2019. "Arion Long on Changing Feminine Care–The Embrace Ambition Series." *YouTube* video. https://www.youtube.com/watch?v=46tyWLg9YTA.

- UN Women. *Policy Brief: The Impact of COVID-19 on Women.* New York, 2020 Accessed October 29, 2020. https://www.un.org/sexualviolenceinconflict/wp-content/uploads/2020/06/report/policy-brief-the-impact-of-covid-19-on-women/policy-brief-the-impact-of-covid-19-on-women-en-1.pdf

- Wilson, Heather. "Brave Through Grief: An Interview with Arion Long." *YouTube* video, 22:35, May 9, 2020. https://www.youtube.com/watch?v=esHXHCMOzoQ.

CHAPTER 8—MAKE A PLAN FOR SURVIVING THE "TERRIBLE TWOS"

- Brustein, Darrah. 2016. "The 20 Hardest Things About Starting a Business." *Business Collective.* https://businesscollective.com/the-20-hardest-things-about-starting-a-business/.

- Contee, Cheryl. *Mechanical Bull: How You Can Achieve Startup Success.* Lioncrest Publishing, 2019.

- Daniel, Brandice. 2019. "The Real Winners Are on the Outside." Filmed March 6, 2019 in Memphis. TEDxMemphis video, 13:13. https://www.ted.com/talks/brandice_daniel_the_real_winners_are_on_the_outside.

- Raz, Guy, host. "Spanx- Sara Blakely." How I Built This with Guy Raz (podcast). July 2, 2017. Accessed September 27, 2020. https://www.npr.org/2017/08/15/534771839/spanx-sara-blakely.

CHAPTER 9—CREATE YOUR OWN SERENDIPITY

- Ogunjimi, Gbenga. *Borderless Voice: The Power of Telling Your Story and Defining Your Identity.* Self-published, 2018.

- Zafarris, Jess. 2017. "The Etymology of 'Serendipity.'" Useless Etymology (blog). December 2, 2017. https://uselessetymology.com/2017/12/02/the-etymology-of-serendipity/.

CHAPTER 10—LEAD LIKE A WOMAN

- Dufu, Tiffany and Gloria Steinem. *Drop the Ball: Achieving More by Doing Less.* New York: Flatiron Books, 2018.

- Gerzema, John. 2012. "The Athena Doctrine." *YouTube* video, 15:18. October 1, 2012. https://www.youtube.com/watch?v=YxgTsyL4yoE

- Guerrero, Dorothy. 2020. "Nonprofit Leadership: Is There a Gender Gap?" Mission Box. Accessed June 20, 2020. https://www.missionbox.com/article/127/nonprofit-leadership-is-there-a-gender-gap.

- Mohr, Tara. 2015. *Playing Big: Find Your Voice, Your Mission, Your Message.* New York: Avery, An Imprint of Penguin Random House.

CHAPTER 11—KISS PERFECTIONISM GOODBYE

CHAPTER 12—BE MISSION-DRIVEN, BUT NOT A MARTYR

- Zipkin, Nina. 2018. "Out of $85 Billion in VC Funding Last Year, Only 2.2 Percent Went to Female Founders. And Every Year, Women of Color Get Less Than 1 Percent of Total Funding." *Entrepreneur,* December 12, 2018. https://www.entrepreneur.com/article/324743.

CONCLUSION—DARE LIKE NEVER BEFORE

- "First Round 10 Year Project." n.d. First Round 10 Year Project. Accessed August 29, 2020. http://10years.firstround.com/.

- Olsen, Dana. 2018. "Do Female Founders Get Better Results? Here's What Happened on My Quest to Find out | PitchBook." Pitchbook.Com. January 23, 2018. https://pitchbook.com/news/articles/do-female-founders-get-better-results-heres-what-happened-when-i-tried-to-find-out.

- "Population, Female (% of Total) | Data." 2017. Worldbank. Org. 2017. https://data.worldbank.org/indicator/SP.POP.TOTL. FE.ZS.

ACKNOWLEDGMENTS

———

If you read all the way through this book to the end and have landed on this page, you should be acknowledged. It's been quite a journey writing this book. It almost didn't happen dozens of times. My biggest accomplishment was sitting still long enough to get all of these thoughts out of my head and onto a laptop. Doing so meant being quieter and more absent than usual in the lives of loved ones. To all of my friends and family who encouraged my writing process, edited my words, and edified my soul every step of the way, I am forever grateful.

Holdjiny, my love, I believe you have earned a round of applause. You had a front-row seat to all the ugly crying, gnashing of the teeth, procrastination, and long nights. There would be no book without your patience, love, and willingness to survive on takeout for weeks.

Dave and Neapolis, you were the first people who made room for me to dare, regardless of what it cost you. Thanks for being my amazing parents and champions.

Dr. Ronnie, you have been my quiet benefactor, a consistent voice of reason, a trusted advisor, and an inspiration. You remind me to find joy in everything and to never settle for less than exceptional. Every daring girl should be blessed to have an uncle like you.

Adia, I had some nerve asking you (a physician, a newlywed, and first-time mom) to read my whole book and give comments—and during a pandemic, no less! Thanks for always making me better. I couldn't have done this without you, and I wouldn't dare try.

To the team at New Degree Press, thank you for providing a platform to bring my book to life. Eric Koester, Brian Bies, Cass Lauer, and Leah Pickett deserve special thanks. No one has done more to make this book happen, though, than Julie Colvin. You are the heroine of this publishing story. Thanks for your calming presence, your sharp eye, your steady commitment to keeping me accountable to myself, and your constant reassurance.

This book was made possible also by a community of people who believed in me so fervently they preordered their copies and helped promote the book before it even went to print. Thanks to you all, many of whom read my early manuscript and gave input on the book title and cover. You are amazing, and as promised you are in the book (listed in alphabetical order by first name):

Adrian Hopkins
Ajuah Helton
Alberta McKnight
Amy Jacobus
Andreina Munoz
Annette Raveneau
Ayanna Smith
Ben Wilkes
Callan Blount Fleming
Charisse Williams
Chevon Deputy
Daniel Horgan
Dave Smith
Dawn Foster
Deborah Pierre
DeDee Cai
Dionne Smith
Dr. Kumba Hinds Murray
Dr. Ronnie Jones
Eduardo Placer
Erin Perkins
Estela Lauredan
Genevia Sawyer
Heather O'Neill
Holdjiny Toussaint
Isha James
Jaime Banks
Jazmine Davis
Jhanique Prince
Joanna Seltzer
Justine Bassett
Kathleen St. Louis Caliento

Kathryn Flynn
Keely Smith
Keisha Brown
Kristine Sloan
Laura Donald
Lauren Booker Allen
Liz Miller
Maria Martineau
Keith Smith Jr.
Neapolis Smith
Nita Baum
Pamela Rogers
Ronnie Coleman
Samira Cook Gaines
Shani Grell